YEAR IN, YEAR OUT

E·P·DUTTON & CO. INC.
1852   1952
CELEBRATING 100 YEARS OF PUBLISHING

BY THE SAME AUTHOR

Novels

CHLOE MARR
ONCE ON A TIME
THE RED HOUSE MYSTERY
MY PIM PASSES BY
TWO PEOPLE
FOUR DAYS' WONDER

Light Articles

THE DAY'S PLAY
THE HOLIDAY ROUND
ONCE A WEEK
THE SUNNY SIDE

Essays

NOT THAT IT MATTERS
IF I MAY
BY WAY OF INTRODUCTION

Children's Books

WHEN WE WERE VERY YOUNG
WINNIE-THE-POOH
NOW WE ARE SIX
THE HOUSE AT POOH CORNER

Plays

FIRST PLAYS
SECOND PLAYS
THREE PLAYS
FOUR PLAYS
THE IVORY DOOR
MICHAEL AND MARY
TOAD OF TOAD HALL
MISS ELIZABETH BENNET

Verse

FOR THE LUNCHEON INTERVAL
BEHIND THE LINES
THE NORMAN CHURCH

General

PEACE WITH HONOUR

Autobiography

IT'S TOO LATE NOW

Stories

BIRTHDAY PARTY
A TABLE NEAR THE BAND

YEAR IN, YEAR OUT

by

A. A. MILNE

with decorations by

E. H. SHEPARD

NEW YORK: E. P. DUTTON & CO. INC.

Library of Congress Catalog Card Number: 52-10441

To D. M.

[*'The Daphnes look best when planted in bold groups
in the border.'*]

Of the Daphnes to group in a border
Authorities call the attention
To *Mezereon* first, then *Cneorum,*
Blagayana (these forming a quorum),
With others, no matter the order,
Too many to mention;
But none of the books in my Gardening shelf
Gives the Daphne I love—looking sweet by herself.

Preface to the American Edition

As I have explained in the first chapter, I have found a place in this book (which might be described as autobiographical table-talk) for a number of contributions to various reviews and magazines over the preceding years. There may be readers who are glad to meet again some such article or set of verses which they happened to like at the time but had now forgotten; equally there may be readers who prefer to spend their money, or exercise their borrowing powers, in a book entirely new to them. For the benefit, or otherwise, of American readers it might be as well to say that only in the month of January will they come across anything which has had a previous existence on their side of the Atlantic.

A. A. MILNE

Cotchford Farm
HARTFIELD, SUSSEX

*A*RS, as we have been told too often, *est celare artem*, which means that good craftsmanship should conceal artifice. This is true of all writing, but for creative writing I would add *Res est celare rem*, by which I mean that it is the business of the writer to hide the fact that writing is his business. Readers are not interested in the mechanics of authorship. They do not attack their favourite stories with a better appetite by knowing how and why they were written; any more than they increase the enjoyment of their favourite food by the knowledge, now apparently inescapable, of its vitamin-content. A lagoon in the Pacific, however misconceived, can be pictured happily by a library-subscriber in Peckham; but the picture loses both probability and charm if it comprehends an author on the foreshore looking up lagoons in his encyclopaedia. Doubtless the reader knows at the back of his mind that the book has an author, just as the playgoer knows at the back of his mind that King Lear has a television set. But the knowledge should remain in the background while the entertainment is on, else the illusion will be lost.

This, however, only applies to creative writing. For the

sort of book in which the author is not behind the curtain pulling the strings, but in the glare of the footlights displaying his personality, there can be no pretence. You are asked now to be interested, not in the adventures of d'Artagnan nor in the absurdities of Mr Pumblechook, but in the ideas, beliefs and prejudices of the man on the title-page; a person no less real than, if by no means as attractive as, Elizabeth Bennet. So, whatever of entertainment this book is going to offer (and at this stage I am as ill-equipped to judge the matter as the reader), nothing will be lost by a confession of its origins.

Of all the foolish things which Dr Johnson said, the most foolish was: 'No man but a blockhead ever wrote, except for money.' What he should have said was that a writer, having written what pleased him, was a blockhead if he did not sell it in the best market. But a writer wants something more than money for his work: he wants permanence. However highly rewarded the ephemeral life of newspaper or magazine may be, he still yearns for the immortality, even if only in the British Museum, of stiff covers.

In the days when I wrote what I liked to think of as a humorous article every week, it was easy to put the best fifty out of each hundred into covers; as it was also with the weekly essays to which I was indentured for a time. But now I have only a drawer full of oddments: casual contributions over the years in many kinds: some, I think, worth preserving, many not: those for which I should like to make provision lacking something, both of quantity and homogeneity, for a book. So I have found a place for these in this calendar of disconnected thoughts and memories, such as I have often thought it would be pleasant to keep. Call the whole a pulpit from which to preach, a platform from which to talk, a stage on which to play the fool, or something of all three; in fact, regard it as a setting for a Variety Performance on the Author's Benefit Night, which will take place even if the author sits solitary, but not unrewarded, in an empty house.

The farmhouse wherein we live is a very old one. None can say exactly how old; but because it is still marked as a farm in the ordnance map, so it is still known. It had been more or less derelict for some years before we came. The lovely old house could be made habitable, and a barn turned into a garage with rooms for a gardener above it, but most of the outbuildings were as forlorn as Mariana; and as they gradually fell to pieces we used the wood and the bricks for other purposes, and let such fields to a neighbouring farmer as we were not going to make into a garden. For ourselves we have bred no more than goldfish and fattened no more than a few pigs.

One day during the war, having to be in London for various reasons, I went into a large store to buy a sponge. We pumped our own water at that time, so we could not complain of its quality, but it was death to sponges. All the springs in these parts have iron in them, and the iron enters into the soul of the sponge, making the yellow, as Macbeth was saying, one red; after which the whole thing disintegrates.

The price of a sponge has always come as something of a shock to me. Sponges don't look expensive, as does a charmingly coloured piece of soap embossed *Rêve d'Amour*. They have a ragged, uncared-for appearance, as if their owner had never taken any pride in them. One feels that one should get for one's money something more regular in shape, with fewer holes in it. It is true that sponges live at the bottom of the sea, which makes the overhead considerable, but there seems to be no lack of them. The love-life of a sponge is not a subject on which one can ponder for long without becoming un-settled; enough to know that in course of time, and after some pretty confusion by the bride when hinting at the possibility, they have small sponges. And so the breed goes on. A static life, I have often thought, being a sponge; but, of course, an absorbing one.

I chose a large, healthy specimen, once, no doubt, the pride of the reef. Its price was wired on to it; otherwise I should have supposed the figure to be a rough valuation of the department, or possibly the whole store. When I had made the necessary calculations, 'this way and that dividing the swift mind'—banker, solicitor, stockbroker—I gave the assistant my name and address.

The girl's face lit up. This does happen sometimes, and on the rare occasions when it does, my face lights up too. It was pleasant to think that she had read my books, or (more prob-ably) knew somebody who had. We smiled at each other in a friendly way, and she said that I must be feeling proud of myself. I gave a modest imitation of a man who prefers to have it said rather than to say it.

'Taking a holiday now?' she asked.

This puzzled me a little. One need not take a long holiday in order to buy a sponge; and, of course, if one had known the price, one would have known that one couldn't afford to. There was no reason why I shouldn't have left my heroine in my hero's arms, dashed to London, bought sponge, and dashed back in time to hear her say: 'Oh, darling, I never dreamed it would be like this!' However, I gave her another smile, and went to another department to buy a pair of slippers.

It was to a man this time that I gave my name. His face also lit up; so, of course, did mine. Never before had I been such a public character. He said:

'Well, you've been doing a fine bit of work.'

Had I known him better, I should have asked him to which manifesto or pamphlet he was referring, for one likes to be told these things. As it was, I said with a shrug: 'Oh well, we must all do what we can.'

He agreed.

'Got it all in?' he went on.

This baffled me. It seemed to be, but could hardly be, a low reference to the nominal fee which I accept sometimes for these things. But, before I could answer, he added—and so put the afternoon at last in its true perspective:

'We owe a lot to you farmers.'

After all these years of authorship it is disheartening to find that it is not one's name but one's address which raises admiration in the breasts of strangers. Yet if one is to be mistaken for what one is not, I would as soon be thought a farmer as anything. I was to make a speech once at a City dinner, and the stranger next to my wife, having consulted her name-card and the menu, said:

'I see your husband is talking to us tonight. Let me see, isn't he something to do with the Gas, Light and Coke Company?'

That, I think, did me an injustice; the other did not. Indeed I have sometimes played with the idea of making this place a farm again, but the amount of writing which it would involve has stayed me. I do enough writing anyway.

At the beginning of the war the Army wanted to requisition a piece of waste land for which we had never found a use. I made no objection, and was sent a form to fill up, so that a fair rental might be fixed. I had to answer about sixty questions: the acreage of the land, how long I had owned it, what I had paid for it, what crops I had grown on it; its value as grassland if I hadn't ploughed it up, its value as ploughland if I didn't use it for grazing; my rotation of crops for the last six years; the average profit I should expect from turnips, from swedes, from oats, from raspberries, from chickens, from curly-kale; my outgoings on artificial manures—there were spaces for all these things and many more.

I just couldn't think of the answers. All it grew, besides bracken and bramble, was cowslips. After sleepless days and nights and many false beginnings, I wrote diagonally across the form: 'I give you the thing.' I had a most charming letter of thanks in return; I didn't know that Government departments could be so grateful.

It is in youth that birthdays matter most, and I was unlucky in that mine came in the middle of January. School began on the Wednesday in the week 15th–22nd, perhaps the unhappiest week of the year, as the Lent Term was the dullest term; and to have one's birthday dropped into such a week was to rob it of all its natural delight. It may have been, too, that there was something of a hangover after Christmas in the pockets of my family. 'What, *again*?' one can imagine them saying. 'Why, we gave him a bicycle only the other day!' In any case, the second bicycle, if such it proved to be, could only come into play in three months' time, a hardly realizable future, when Heaven would re-open anyway, bicycles or no bicycles. Moreover, there I was at school with half a dozen letters and no time on my hands, and anxious parents asking by every post if I had written to thank Uncle Tom yet.

One of the reasons why a man should marry is to have this business of polite letter-writing taken off his hands; the thank-you-very-muches and the so-sorry-we-can't-comes. Women have a sense of duty in these matters which men lack; perhaps because they interchange little gifts more readily than men. It is for this reason that I address more particularly to them a dissertation on

THE ART OF SAYING THANKYOU

Just at first it is easy.

'What do you *say*, darling?' prompts Nanny, with a showman's air of 'Now listen to this,' but a little anxiously in case the thing misses fire; and there are Daddy and Mummy hovering, Mummy having set the scene with a 'Well, *isn't* that kind of Auntie?'; and there is Aunt Ethel waiting with a self-conscious smile, and rather wishing now that she had sprung another three-and-six and bought the one on wheels; and everything in nature is telling you that this is the moment for your set speech.

'Tankoo,' you gulp. You can hardly miss it.

Later, when you have to do it all for yourself, it is more difficult.

Let us consider first the gratitude which is expressed by word of mouth. This admits of much less variation than written thanks, and need not keep us long. All that it demands is spontaneity. The schoolboy's 'Oo, I say, thanks *frightfully*' sets the standard. It is difficult to better this, though you may throw in an awed 'Coo!' if you feel that it comes naturally to you. At the same time you must be careful not to overdo it. Some presents may almost be said to manufacture their own response; no young woman receiving a diamond clip from Uncle George, no young man contemplating a set of matched irons, will need to think of the words. They will bubble out automatically, and, however illiterate and repetitive, they will be the right ones. But if Uncle George has merely given you another white elephant for the mantelpiece, spontaneity will get you nowhere. Fade out at once that high ecstatic note on which you were starting, for you will never keep it up. Just throw your arms round his neck, make a face over it (if you must) at your husband, cry 'Oh, Uncle George, *what* can I say?'—and don't say it.

Many years ago my House subscribed for a wedding present to a form-master who was getting married. He made a charming speech of thanks, whose opening words will never be forgotten by those who heard it. 'I shall value this,' he boomed, 'not only for its intrinsic worth, which must be *enormous* . . .' He had a way, much imitated in private by the humorists of his form, of drawing out the final 's' in a word, and by the time he had finished with it the intrinsic worth of that electro-plated tea-tray was very enormous indeed. That is what I mean by overdoing it. In similar circumstances it is a good rule to make sure about the lion first, if this can be done without ostentation.

But it is an impertinence in me to tell you how to express your thanks orally, for nobody, I am sure, could do it more charmingly and more tactfully than yourself. Written thanks, however, are another matter. *Littera scripta manet*, if you happen to know what that means; and it is possible that your grateful little letter, having gone the round of the breakfast-table, will be preserved in some time-resisting form, either as a wedge for the scullery window, or, more respectfully, to mark the place in Aunt Ethel's library book, *Hearts Asunder*. In the latter case a wider public is immediately secured for it. It would not be at all to your liking to know that a week later some strange woman in Bexhill might be reading the little note you dashed off so hastily, and condemning you as illiterate.

Do not, therefore, pour out your gratitude in the first words which come into your head. They may turn out to be these:

DARLING AUNT ETHEL,

Thank you so very much for the very sweet little box of hand-kerchiefs, it is very kind of you, just the very kind I wanted, because I was getting very short, how very sweet of you! With my very best love to you and Uncle George and again my very best thanks,

Your very loving
ROSEMARY

A charming letter; but if you re-read it, as you always should, you will feel vaguely that there is something wrong with it.

'Am I not,' you will ask yourself, 'overworking the word "very"?' Well, quite frankly, you are.

'What of Bexhill?' you will wonder. 'Will it not be raising its eyebrows?' Undoubtedly Bexhill will be doing just that.

But now suppose you go to the other extreme; suppose you decide to make your letter a work of art from which Aunt Ethel will never let herself be separated. For instance:

Aunt Ethel, darling, all my thanks
For that delightful box of hanks,
So many and so dainty too,
My favourite, perhaps, the blue,
The *sweetest* shade—but no, I think
I'm craziest about the pink,
And one can hardly choose between
The lilac and the apple green!
I don't know *which* I like the most!
And now, in haste to catch the post,
And hoping Uncle George is better,
I close this rather hurried * letter
With once again a thousand thanks
For that delightful box of hanks.

(**Poetic licence.   *It took you the whole morning.*)

One could hardly express gratitude more gracefully. But what will happen? Aunt Ethel will be so delighted at having such a *literary* niece that she will copy the letter out and send it to her more distant friends, inevitably leaving out some of the words. Moreover, she will recite it to visitors over the tea-table, interrupting herself at every third line with 'Let me see, *how* did it go?' or 'No, *that's* wrong. Wait a moment, I shall get it directly.' Now poetry in which some of the words are left out is never quite the same thing; and it cannot bear interruption. You will have done yourself no good at all. *Medio tutissimus ibis* (if you know anybody who can translate it for you); 'Literate, not literary' should be your motto.

But let us consider a more difficult form of letter. It is well known that wedding-presents do not always find a permanent resting-place at once, but, in some obstinate cases, travel around from home to home before settling down in the spare-room. It may happen that, being yourself newly be-trothed, you will receive from an absent-minded married

friend the identical ornamental match-box which you chose
so carefully for her own wedding present two years before.
How shall you thank her for it? You don't want to be rude
—at least, you do want to, naturally, but you think it would
be inadvisable—and yet you don't want her to get away with
it altogether.

So:

DARLING SHEILA

How sweet of you, I simply love it. I saw one exactly like it at
Peter Jones two years ago, and positively yearned for it, but had
to give it to a friend who was getting married, and have been
regretting it ever since. Now I have really got it for myself, and
you can imagine how pleased I am.

Your fondest

ROSEMARY

This is where Sheila goes hot all over suddenly and begins
wondering . . . which presumably is what you wanted.

Another problem which arises is when your Uncle Henry,
from whom you have expectations, writes to say that he is
sending you an old Venetian goblet which he picked up in
Venice, and the postman has dropped it in the Brompton
Road, so that this time it is picked up in 57 pieces, as you discover when you unpack the parcel. If you just write gratefully back to Uncle Henry, saying how beautiful it is, he will
expect to see it in all its glory when next he comes to dinner.
If you tell him that it was *sweet* of him to think of you all that
way away, and it sounded *too* divine, but *unfortunately* it
arrived in 57 pieces, he will be extremely annoyed, and
suspect that you broke it yourself when unpacking it. So
what can you do?

This baffled me for a long time, and at first I thought that
there was nothing for it but emigration. But now I have

discovered the answer. You write him one of your perfectly charming letters, saying how much you are looking forward to the arrival of the goblet; and you add that, by an extra-ordinary coincidence, you have just sent *him* a rather sweet little piece of Dresden china which you picked up in Dresden. You then go out and buy a rather sweet little piece of Dresden china in South Kensington, break it into 57 pieces, and address the result to him. All you have to do now is to sit back and wait to see what *he* does.

Finally (for I do not wish to overtax you) there is the bread-and-butter letter, or, as it is sometimes called, the 'Collins'. Mr Collins, as you may remember (but I should doubt it), left Longbourn with the promise to his host: 'You will speedily receive from me a letter of thanks for every mark of your regard during my stay in Hertfordshire,' and hosts and hostesses in every county have been expecting such letters speedily ever since.

Now it is just because our hostess is expecting it that the more artistic natures, like yours and mine, find a difficulty in writing. To acknowledge gratefully a box of handkerchiefs is another matter; it is our first opportunity to say Thank you, and the natural impulse is there. But when we said good-bye to our hostess on Monday morning, we poured out our thanks (I hope) for every mark of her regard during our stay in Buckinghamshire, and we have no spontaneous impulse to repeat it on Monday evening. Such a repetition, formal and expected, is, we feel, meaningless.

I make, therefore, the following suggestions:

1. *Don't* be speedy. Wait a few days; thus giving the impression that this is not a Collins, but an irresistible expression of emotion recollected in tranquillity, which you struggled, in vain, to keep under.

2. Leave your tooth-brush behind, apologize profoundly, and so pass naturally on to 'And, while I am writing, may I once again . . .'

If you think this out, you will see that these are alternative methods of approach. To use them simultaneously would be to create a false impression.

And there I shall leave it, hoping that I have been helpful. You need not thank me. This sort of writing is its own reward.

To turn to another sort of writing. Charles Lutwidge Dodgson was born on January 27th, 1832, became a mathematical lecturer at Oxford in 1855, and was ordained deacon in 1861. Mathematical lecturers joke with difficulty; clergymen with lamentable ease. The combination does not seem promising. We picture Don Dodgson and Deacon Dodgson setting out together to amuse the Liddell girls, and for all the brightness of the day we shudder. But this was one of those enchanted afternoons when anything may happen. A fairy wand touched Don and Deacon, and magically they became Lewis Carroll; the three little girls became magically a million little girls, a million little boys, big girls, big boys, men and women; and there was born on a golden afternoon nearly ninety years ago Alice, of Wonderland and the Looking Glass.

But don't suppose that this strange Lewis Carroll was now trying to amuse a world-audience, or that he was thinking, when once he had put pen to paper, of his Liddell girls. He was writing solely to amuse the strange Lewis Carroll, this childlike person whom he had suddenly discovered in himself. Sometimes one of the old Dodgsons would elbow his way in and insist on being amused too. Then would come prolonged aquatic jokes about 'feathering' and 'catching crabs', such as would appeal to an unathletic deacon and be the occasion of sycophantic laughter from a nice little girl.

Turn to the 'Wool and Water' chapter in the *Looking Glass*, and listen carefully to the conversation between the Sheep and Alice in the boat. The Reverend Dodgson is at large. Turn to the next chapter and listen to Humpty Dumpty:

'When *I* use a word,' Humpty Dumpty said in rather a scornful tone, 'it means just what I choose it to mean—neither more nor less.'

'The question is,' said Alice, 'whether you can make words mean different things.'

'The question is,' said Humpty Dumpty, 'which is to be master —that's all . . . Impenetrability! That's what *I* say.'

Lewis Carroll is back again. The Deacon has vanished with the suddenness which is such a feature of the country.

But it must have been the Don who insisted afterwards on making the stories into dreams.

'My dear fellow,' he said to Carroll, 'a human child couldn't go down a rabbit-hole. Consider for a moment the relative sizes of the aperture and the intruding body. And, in any case, rabbits do not talk, and what's all this about substituting a flamingo for a croquet-mallet? Have you ever observed the Common Flamingo—*Phoenicopterus Antiquorum*? Think carefully for a moment and you will see that the whole thing is absurd. Now, if it had been Alice's *dream*— well, we all know what ridiculous things happen in dreams. Only last night I dreamed that I was giving a lecture on Determinants in my night-shirt, before, of all people, the late Prince Consort, when suddenly——'

And Lewis Carroll rubbed his head in a bewildered way and said sadly, 'No, it couldn't have happened, could it? You know, just for a moment I thought it did. Somewhere . . . somehow . . . Oh, well.' So it became (how wrongly, how stupidly) a dream and, being a work of genius, managed to survive it.

For who is ever interested in somebody else's dream? Do we think of Alice as a little girl who ate too much pudding for dinner and had a nightmare in the afternoon? We can all do that for ourselves.

But Alice is that real little girl who, alone of all little girls, has had tea with the March Hare and the Mad Hatter, and played croquet with the Queen of Hearts; who has had 'Jabberwocky' explained to her by Humpty Dumpty, and heard Tweedledee recite 'The Walrus and the Carpenter'; the child who walked into the setting sun by the side of the White Knight, that gentle, foolish, fond old man, with whom, in some literary Valhalla, Mr Dick flies kites—special kites, kites not now of Mr Dick's invention.

'I was wondering what the mouse-trap was for,' said Alice. 'It isn't likely that there would be any mice on the horse's back.'

'Not very likely, perhaps,' said the Knight, 'but if they *do* come, I don't choose to have them running all about.'

O happy Carroll! O blessed Knight! Did Alice dream that? Listen:

Years afterwards she could bring the whole scene back again, as if it had been only yesterday—the mild blue eyes and kindly smile of the Knight—the setting sun gleaming through his hair and shining on his armour in a blaze of light—the horse quietly moving about, with the reins hanging loose on his neck, cropping the grass at her feet—and the black shadows of the forest behind.

There you have Lewis Carroll giving the lie to the Dodgsons. It was no dream, no story for children. It happened. He was there himself.

I have emphasized the absurdity of the dream-convention, because it is Alice who has kept the books in the hearts of children, Alice of whom children would expect real adventures, not dreams. But it is also Alice who was responsible for the occasional intrusions of the Dodgsons: the chop-logic of the Don, the over-easiness of the Deacon. They never could resist a little girl. In *The Hunting of the Snark* there is no little girl, and the result is undiluted Carroll, the most inspired nonsense in the language. Had he written no more than the *Snark* and *The Walrus and the Carpenter*, he would have deserved immortality.

But he would not have got it. He needed Alice to hold his hand. She is not pretty, as drawn by Tenniel; she has no great charm of manner; but, because she is a real child, wherever her piping voice is heard, children will follow, and at their heels will troop the grown-ups, eager to see what strange new company she is keeping. Look! Now she is talking to a man on a horse! Observe the spiked anklets round the horse's feet. That is to guard against the bites of Sharks. It is the rider's own invention. . . .

Many years ago I wrote a short story which never got beyond the typist to whom first it was sent. In this story somebody, a doctor presumably, gave a lecture on 'The Use and Abuse of Corsets', or possibly was qualified as the sort of man who gave that sort of lecture. I have no idea now why he came into the story, nor what the story was about. All I do remember is that in the typed version the title of the lecture was given as 'The Ox and Abux of Corsets'.

This worried me for weeks. I tried to get into the mind of the typist, who surely must know more about foundation garments than I, and who thought that a pair of stays might have both an Ox *and* an Abux. My writing, no doubt, had its moments of illegibility, but 'use and abuse' is a well-worn conjunction, and I felt that she should have made a more likely guess at it. There is something about an 'abux of corsets' suggestive of a window-display in Regent Street, but the ox gets us nowhere. Which was where the story got

Now I suggest (and this is my only contribution to the Higher Criticism) that a misprint in one of Lewis Carroll's books did get him somewhere. I suggest that when the White Knight said that his horse's anklets were 'to guard against the bites of sharks', the compositor in his first proof made the very easy substitution of an 'n' for an 'h', and set Carroll wondering what 'the bites of snarks' were like . . . wondering, until inevitably *The Hunting of the Snark* followed. Which is the way such things get written.

We called him Berry, because he was brown as a berry, and because his mother was Sherry. He was a golden cocker. All the goodness and badness, the tricks ingratiating and infuriating, all the charm and the pathos which has mounted up in literature, descriptive of this or that particular dog, from puppyhood to old age, are to be found in every cocker spaniel. He knows it all, he has it all, he does it all. In his relations with man every other dog plagiarizes him. In his relations with literature he is the inevitable plagiarist. So if

something is to be said of him, let it be said in verse, where
the manner at least can be one's own.

Here he is on his first birthday:

What are we to do with Berry?
  Well, it's undecided yet.
When he's bad, he's very, very,
  When he's good, he's just a pet.

Did his father's father's father
  Wed a wolf beneath the rose,
Thus accounting for his rather
  Savage temper? Heaven knows.

Was his mother's mother's mother
  Boarded with a rural dean,
Which explains, we tell each other,
  Why his temper's so serene?

Was his auntie's auntie's auntie
  Just a cur whom cats could cow?
Even so, we say, why can't he
  Show a little courage now?

Courage? Why, at times a dozen
  Lions aren't as brave as he,
And his cousin's cousin's cousin
  Shows a hero's pedigree.

Fierce he is, and very gentle,
  Brave and coward, good and bad;
And, which may be accidental,
  Now and then completely mad.

Do we love him? No, we nearly
  Hate him, he annoys us so.
Hate him? No, we love him dearly,
  And we cannot let him go.

Envoi

Yesterday he bit his missis,
    And I gave him all I'd got.
Back he comes with licks and kisses—
    Well, he's going . . . No, he's not.

He didn't. I wrote those verses one August, and he stayed
with us until the following January, when he was run over.
It was the day before my birthday: a birthday as little for
rejoicing as those earlier ones of which I have written. It was
comforting to say a word of apology to him, a word of
farewell.

I

Long ago, when you were bad,
    I composed a little verse,
Asking if the dog we had
    Were a blessing or a curse.

Naughty nearly all the time,
    Bearable by fits and starts,
Yet you found the way to climb
    Into our uncertain hearts.

When you saw your name in print
    Was it that you understood?
Anyway, you took the hint
    And decided to be good;

Good as gold—in tawny eyes,
    Good as gold—on silky coat,
Making into witless lies
    All the clever things I wrote.

II

Happy not to be alone,
    Yet a little dog prefers
Someone for his very own:
    She was yours and you were hers.

She was yours to guard and love . . .
　　While she's weeding, there you sit,
In your mouth a garden glove,
　　'Just in case she's needing it.'

But the tilted head proclaims
　　With a plea she cannot miss:
'*When* you think it's time for games,
　　Here's a glove; we'll play with this.'

Racing with her round the fields,
　　Watching as she does her hair—
Morn to night the moment yields
　　Something which the two can share.

III

Golden heart, forever still,
　　Golden head, as if asleep . . .
Cars must hurry up the hill,
　　Why should any woman weep?

Not a moment in the day,
　　Not a corner, far or near,
But, remorseless, seems to say:
　　'Here he used to be, and here.'

In the quiet of the wood,
　　Earth for bed and earth for sky,
In the unknown solitude
　　Beauty passes. Let it die.

That was five years ago. And now the wild daffodils have
drifted over his grave, and in a little while there will be
nothing to show where he lies. But he has not been easy to
forget.

A MONG the disadvantages of Central Heating in a sixteenth-century farmhouse in which the doorways never quite reached the ground, and in which the chimneys offered to the stoutest an alternative means of getting in and out: a house, moreover, which never really pulled itself together after two flying-bombs had visited it—one of the disadvantages, I say, is that, at a time when the Minister of Fuel is congratulating householders on their patriotic economy in the use of coke which they haven't got, the cold iron fluting called a radiator becomes a medium of Central Icing besides which the absence of an occasional lump of coal to keep a log fire in being seems of small account. At such a time, in such weather as surrounds and filters through me as I write, February offers nothing to the mind but a profound desire to forget about it. I propose, therefore, to think of something else: something which moves me to a little warmth.

Dickens is said to have amused himself with a shelf of dummy books, suitably titled in gold lettering on the back, such as might be found in any gentleman's library. One of them, which has fixed itself in my memory, was called *Five Minutes in China*. This must have seemed pleasantly silly at the time; but today, when travellers, or fellow-travellers, come back from a fortnight's personally conducted tour of Russia, knowing all the secrets of the country, the title would hardly raise an eyebrow. A lately-returned explorer dispelled the Labour Camp myth finally, with the assurance that even an afternoon's aeroplane trip had failed to disclose one.

The belief that 'proof' can only be established by 'evidence', positive or negative, is a legacy of the law-courts, which holds the evidence of documents, eye-witnesses and experts in greater respect than it holds reason. But, in fact, reason is often the better authority. The evidence which is accepted by the Law is subjective: a witness may be a liar, an expert ignorant, a document forged: but logic can be as objective as mathematics. The dispute between Communists and anti-Communists as to which half of Korea was the aggressor could be continued for ever if it depended (as many seemed to suppose) on the conflicting assertions of North and South Koreans. But it does not. It depends on reason. We start with the premise that a State meditating aggression mobilizes and deploys its troops in readiness for attack; that it chooses both the place and the time for the first assault. *Therefore* it has the advantage of its opponent at the first encounter, and wins the opening battle. The North Koreans won the opening battle. *Therefore* the South Koreans could not have been the aggressors. So, too, we had proof that it was Hitler, not Stalin, who broke the alliance between them

in 1941; not because each accused the other, and one was the
greater liar or more treacherous friend, but because one
immediately advanced and the other retreated.

Now the truth about the Labour Camps in Russia does not
depend on the 'evidence' of the Kremlin on the one side, or
of the escaped prisoner on the other. Still less, of course, does
it depend on the evidence of the returned traveller who didn't
see one. There are millions of Englishmen who have travelled
about their country for years, and never seen a prison, a
Shakespeare play or a Brimstone butterfly. We know that
there are Labour Camps in Russia, because logically there
must be. A Labour Camp is as integral a part of a Communist
State as a secret ballot is of a Democratic State.

For when an Englishman mounts his soap-box in Hyde
Park, or writes a letter to his local paper, and calls upon his
countrymen to 'get rid of this pestilential Government', all
he is urging is that they should vote for the Opposition at the
next Election. But in a Communist State, which allows of no
Opposition, there are only two ways of getting rid of a
pestilential Government: assassination or revolution. Anything said, written or even thought against the Kremlin is
therefore an incitement to bloodshed, and no responsible
Government can afford to ignore it. The inciter must either
be executed, or else put away in some place of safety, where
he is no longer a danger, but preferably, still of some manual
service to the State. In other words, he must be sent to a
Slave Labour Camp. . . .

Lately it has become fashionable to say that Communism
can best be fought by opposing to it the positive policy of the
Welfare State. Communism, we are told, in one of those
metaphors without which politicians would be almost
speechless, only flourishes on the soil of discontent. Once

the world is convinced that under Democracy wages can be higher, hours shorter, housing more spacious and false teeth more abundant, then Communism will no longer be a danger, for it will have nothing to offer.

This seems to me a dangerous doctrine, unjustified by recent history. The answer to Slavery is not free wigs and spectacles, but Freedom. In as far as Communism has ever been a popular movement (and that is not very far), it has been a reaction from tyranny, misgovernment or the severe restrictions on liberty imposed by war. The carrot of better living conditions can be dangled successfully whatever the living conditions are; the whole point of the carrot is that the donkey never reaches it. But the freedom of thought and speech and writing which we enjoy is either there or not there, and if it is there, then there is nothing to promise. Communism will never be a natural growth on the soil of freedom. Instead of outbidding the Kremlin in its own rôle of State provider of benefits, we should emphasize the benefits which the British 'working-man' has won for himself: the right to strike; to choose his job; to absent himself from it if there is a race-meeting or a football-match in the neighbourhood; to say what he likes about the management from the foreman upwards. Everything which subtracts from this weakens us in the fight against Communism. Every restriction on liberty makes liberty seem less inevitable, its loss more natural and less worthy of dispute.

We can see what an insignificant appeal Democratic Welfare makes as an alternative to Communism if we consider the refugees from the Comminform states. Did they escape because food was less plentiful in the East; because they would have Saturdays off in the West; because there was an inadequate Pension scheme attached to their trade? What was their complaint against Communism? Always that they were not free to speak, always that they were afraid.

This reminds me of a story which seems appropriate.

A Norwegian commercial traveller was talking to a Russian commercial traveller whom he had not seen for some time.

'Well,' he said, 'and how are things in your country just now? Not too good, I hear.'

'Oh, one can't complain,' said the Russian.

'You had a very bad harvest, didn't you? I'm afraid that means that food's pretty short again?'

'Oh, well,' said the Russian, 'these things happen. One mustn't complain.'

'And I suppose the housing situation is as bad as ever? Do you still have to share a room with another family?'

The Russian shrugged his shoulders with Russian stolidity.

'You know how it is,' he said. 'Some are lucky, and some not so lucky, one can't complain.'

'Look here, my friend,' said the Norwegian, 'why not be frank with me? What's the point of keeping on saying you "*can't complain*"?'

'Well,' said the Russian bitterly, 'you just try complaining.'

This is the Achilles heel of the monstrous god called Communism: not the fact that it gives economic cause for discontent, but that it allows no discontent to be expressed. It is at this that our arrows should be aimed; it is our own Freedom of Discontent which is our surest weapon.

Unfortunately a positive virtue, however small, seems more potent than a negative virtue, however great; and still more unfortunately, every virtue which has been long enjoyed seems negative, and every new virtue positive. At the beginning of the last war we lived under a barrage of motherly talks from the B.B.C. telling us that, as an inspiration to victory, we must proclaim our New Order for Europe. Then, and only then, we should be fighting (positively) *for* something, not just (negatively) against something. Indeed, it began to seem that we were engaged in some sort of civil war for improved social conditions, in which a few foreigners had accidentally got involved. One prominent Liberal was moved to write to *The Times*, saying 'This war is not being fought by our countrymen to get back to the 1930's, and the great majority of them would doubt its being worth winning if it were.' This was as great a libel on his countrymen as on (one hopes) his own humanity and intelligence. For the difference between England in 1930 and any Utopia conceivable by man was infinitely less than the difference between England in 1930 and England under Hitler; or between Democracy and Communism. If any Englishman thought that it was not worth fighting to save himself, and to rescue others, from the Gestapo's torture camps, it would need a good deal more than the present meat ration and housing accommodation to inspire him.

If a centenarian were asked to what he attributed his long life, he might answer 'The health I inherited,' or, more specifically, the beer he had or hadn't drunk, hard work, early rising, cold baths and constant exercise. He would never think of saying 'To the correct mixture of nitrogen and oxygen in the air.' Just as we take existence for granted, so we take freedom of thought, freedom of speech, freedom of writing; without which health, wealth, a good conscience, even life itself, can avail little.

On this question of 'evidence':

Some years ago I wrote a small piece of fiction called 'The Shakespearean Theory', which showed, by extracts from his diary, how Shakespeare came to write Bacon's works. He had felt the need to curb his irrepressible flow of blank verse by dieting himself in the evenings on short prose essays. When he had written enough to make a book of them, like every author he wanted to make a book of them. But, like every manager, publisher and critic, Burbage disapproved of versatility. Let a dramatist stick to his last. So Shakespeare decided to publish his book pseudonymously. In those days, however, a book wasn't published until the author had collected an advance subscription list, and this was something which could hardly be done under a false name. It was necessary, therefore, to find some real person who would father the book for him. What were the qualifications necessary for such fatherhood?

1. The supposed author must be considered sufficiently capable of writing such a book to arouse no suspicion that he was acting as cover for another author.

2. He must have both a reputation and a circle of acquaintance solid enough to ensure a good subscription list.

3. He must be not unreasonably scrupulous.

Bacon, once met, was the obvious man. He accepted the proposal, and Shakespeare got to work upon 'The Advancement of Learning'.

Now factually that story is untrue. Shakespeare did not write Bacon. But its artistic truth is beyond question. That is to say, if we call the dramatist Smith and the lawyer Brown, a story on those lines would be acceptable: as a story of a situation which might have arisen, of events which might have happened, and of people who might so have behaved.

The Baconians, who hold that, on the contrary, it was Bacon who wrote Shakespeare, have given us what they consider to be factual evidence of their theory: anagrams, cryptograms, parallel passages and the like: but they have never offered us any artistic evidence. They have never re-created for us the true story of the Great Imposture. They have begun at the wrong end; trying to prove that it did happen before they had proved that it might have happened.

The true—and by that I mean artistically true—story of how Bacon came to write *Venus and Adonis, Hamlet* and *A Midsummer Night's Dream*, using Shakespeare's name as cover, will not be an easy one to invent. But we shall do our best. Our first task is to give a convincing explanation of the need for anonymity. The usual one is that the theatre was little thought of in those days, and that any traffic with it would be no recommendation for an ambitious young man, earn-estly seeking political favour from an influential uncle. This is good as far as it goes. Winston Churchill's career survived an early novel, but it is doubtful if Mr Attlee would have reached 10 Downing Street had he been known as the author of *Getting Gertie's Garter*. Poetry, however, is another matter. If Essex, Raleigh, Sidney and even Elizabeth herself were not ashamed to acknowledge their own verses, it is difficult to see why Bacon should have been so shy of *Venus and Adonis*. 'Shy' is too mild a word; he was terrified: so terrified that even after his disgrace, when all political and legal ambition was cast aside for ever, he did not dare to confess his author-ship. No, not even on his deathbed could the truth be left to posterity, save by way of anagram and cryptogram. There are Baconians who say that this was because he was the illegitimate son of Elizabeth, and that consequently (if you are following me) the whole realm would have been shaken to its foundations had he been known as the author of *Much Ado About Nothing*. In the first five chapters of our novel we shall be making this a little clearer to you; for the moment let us all agree that Bacon's authorship of the poems and plays had to be Top Secret.

In Chapter 6 Bacon is wondering what to do about it. He has *Venus and Adonis* and *Love's Labour's Lost* in his desk, and somehow he must get them before the public. How? In any creative writing the author tries to put himself into the minds of his characters and then to ask himself: 'What should *I* have done as So-and-so in such-and-such circumstances?' Well, if we had written *In Memoriam* and *Charley's Aunt*, and were the illegitimate son of Queen Victoria, we should have called ourself ffrancis ffoljambe ffoliot, or (in soberer mood) George Hake. In the less crowded world of letters in which he lived Bacon may have feared that an unidentifiable Hake would have been too obvious a pseudonym. If the whole of London were saying: 'Who *is* Hake?' and never getting an answer, might not a speculative eye be turned at last on the trembling Bacon? It might. The risk could not be taken. The only safe way was to present the verses and plays under a real name, whose owner would accept all responsibility, and himself be accepted everywhere as the author.

Which being so, Bacon looked round London, saw a fellow holding a horse outside the Globe Theatre, and chose Will Shakespeare.

Will Shakespeare! The country bumpkin, as Baconians never weary of calling him; the illiterate lout; the butcher's son turned poacher; who could just write his own name, but still had difficulty in spelling it: this poor rustic clod was to convince the world that he had written the masterpieces of the greatest mind of the age. It seems a curious choice to have made, a strange way of keeping a Top Secret; but Chapters 7–10 (I hope) will explain just why the super-intelligent Bacon knew so surely that the super-illiterate Shakespeare was the man for the job. We shall do our best. . . .

But it was not enough to know that an illiterate lout could act convincingly the part of a literary genius. One had also to be assured of his complete integrity. No atomic secret such as our British Communists hand over to Russia as part of their routine was so combustible as the knowledge that Bacon had written *Two Gentlemen of Verona*. How could one be sure that Shakespeare would not sell the secret to Spain, and so (see above) disintegrate the realm; or, even worse, levy blackmail from Bacon on it? The ex-poacher now held the lawyer in what later dramatists were to call the hollow of his hand.

We shall give the answer in Chapters 11 and 12. It was only after many ingenious tests of the fellow's honesty that Bacon was satisfied. Sometimes, suitably disguised, he would send Will off to the Temple with a message and a well-filled purse to deliver, offering to hold his horse for him until he came back. Does Shakespeare betray his trust, and surrender even the sorriest-looking horse for the prospect of escaping with the stranger's gold? Not he! When a Stratford lad holds a horse, he holds a horse. Later I see Bacon swearing him to secrecy, and then telling him some earlier piece of literary gossip which even now would disjoint Kent from the rest of England: as that Chaucer was the illegitimate daughter of Richard II and Maid Marian. And Honest Will, mouth agape, never having heard of any of them, nods vigorously and says: 'Trust Oi, Maister.' . . . And at last Bacon is satisfied, and decides to trust him.

But even now (Chap. 13), while Bacon is saying: 'Well, it's like this. I have written a thing called *Venus and Adonis*, and I want *you*——' a further doubt assails him. As the re-puted author of *The Merry Wives of Windsor*, Shakespeare will frequent the Mermaid tavern. However honest he may have proved himself when sober, who knows how garrulous he might not be in his cups? With a flagon of sack inside him, and another in front of him, might he not hiccup out that he could a tale unfold whose lightest word would harrow up Ben Jonson's soul, freeze Greene's young blood, and make every particular hair of Marlowe stand on end like quills upon a fretful porpentine? When one thought of Her Majesty's shame, of Spain's triumph, of one's own fading chance of the Attorney-Generalship, dare one risk such an unguarded revelation? Honest Will assures him that there is no risk. While little more than a boy at Stratford, he had seduced a young woman in his cups and had been forced to marry her; after which, realizing what the Devil Drink brought a man to, he had taken the pledge and kept it faithfully ever since. All was well. In or out of the Mermaid, Honest Will Shake-speare could be trusted with the Great Secret.

And now just as my publisher, who has read the first thirteen chapters, is happily imagining the Press notices— ('Almost unbearably true to life'—*Stratford Argus*: 'The char-acters live again as we read'—*Leamington Courier*)—I have to confess that Chapter 14 is to present us with the most difficult problem of all; a problem, I fancy, to which Baconians have never really given their minds. The problem is this: *What happened at rehearsals?*

You see, Shakespeare (willy-nilly, so to speak) was always present at rehearsals. However greatly a particular author may dislike hearing his play mangled by actors trying to remember their lines: however completely a particular manager may be convinced that he can misinterpret the play more happily without the author's remonstrance: in this particular case neither had any choice. Shakespeare belonged to the theatre. He was there anyway, as a small-part actor, and, possibly, assistant stage-manager. And now, poor devil, he was supposed to be the author of the play.

I can hear Burbage suggesting that if he had a soliloquy of thirty lines or so just here, 'something about daffodils and violets, Will, old man, sort of thing you do so well', it would help the play along a bit: and another actor asking how the devil he could be expected to get off the stage if the author didn't give him a couplet to take him out: and a third wondering who had annoyed the still-vexed Bermoothes, whoever he was, 'because you know how it is, old boy, if I don't understand what I'm talking about, how can I possibly get it over?': and one of the 'girls' piping, 'Oh, Mr Shakespeare, would you mind if I said the first two lines the other way round, it comes more natural that way, don't you think?'— and poor old Clodhopper, who has never been taught to think, and has no idea what any of them are talking about, blushes and says 'Well, er—I—er—just a moment', and doubles out of the theatre, and doubles across London Bridge, and bursts into the Courts of Justice where Bacon is delivering a judgment, and says 'Excuse me a moment', and then, behind his hand, 'Thirty lines about daffodils and who was Brer Mooses or somebody?' and Bacon adjourns the Court and——

Well, you see what I meant when I said that this chapter was going to be difficult. We shall have to put all we know into it if the *Stratford Argus* is still to call it unbearably true to life. And when we have finished our novel, we shall dedicate it to the memory of a man who has never yet had justice done to him: the greatest actor of his or any age: the most honest and sober citizen: the most loyal and faithful servant: who bore unflinchingly for twenty years the almost impossible burden laid upon him, and never put a foot wrong: the man to whose immortal memory Baconians at their annual dinner should drink a silent toast, but never do: in front of whom, every day of their lives, they should be down on their knees and thank Heaven, fasting, for a good man's service to their hero, but prefer to stand fingers to nose: to the simple countryman who saved Elizabeth from shame, the realm from disintegration, and a lawyer from losing a good job, yet has never been thanked for it: to (no heel-taps, gentlemen)

'WILLIAM SHAKESPEARE!'

This naturally leads me to a consideration of what my friend Mr Harold Appleby-Dodds (of Ambleside) calls 'The Southey MS.'

When Mr Appleby-Dodds heard that I was writing this book, and that all sorts of odd things were getting into it, he generously offered to let me include the extraordinary story which follows. The story falls into five sections, to which, for clarity, I have given headlines. The rest of it is as Mr Appleby-Dodds sent it to me. He has been a little imprecise as to the date on which his great discovery was made, but he assures me that there is a good reason for this.

Here then is the first publication of

THE SOUTHEY MS.

1. *Statement by Harold Appleby-Dodds, Esq., B.A., F.S.A., author of 'With Wordsworth in the Lake District', 'Words-worthiana', 'In the Lake District with Wordsworth', &c.:*

It was in August 19—, while roaming in the hills which look down upon the placid vale of Grasmere, that I discovered the remarkable document which I now make public. The document, consisting of two pages of manuscript, one in prose, the other in verse, lay in a crevice in a little outcrop of rock half-way up the slope of Loughrigg Fell, and it was on my descent that I first noticed it. Assuming it to be something which had slipped out of my pocket on the way up, I replaced it and thought no more of the matter, being concerned only with the business of getting safely down. Indeed, it was not until some years later (19—, to be exact), when cleaning out an old cupboard for the Vicar's jumble sale, that I came across the coat again, and so found myself emptying out the pockets. It was then that for the first time I gave the manuscript my close attention. It was obviously one of considerable importance.

The first page of the MS. spoke for itself, in tones as convincing to me as to any fair-minded person who now reads it. Here it is: one of those graceful introductions so beloved of the poet, explaining the circumstances in which the latest creation of his inspired pen came to be written. Which poet? you ask. Read on, and you will have as little doubt as had I. Read but the title line of the poem, and you will have your clue.

'JONES! WHEN I WALKED WITH YOU AND WILKINSON'

That trumpet voice cannot be mistaken. It is Wordsworth himself who speaks to us.

2. *Wordsworth speaking:*

'JONES! WHEN I WALKED WITH YOU AND WILKINSON'

I distinctly recollect the occasion when these lines were suggested to me. It was in the autumn of 1819 that a gentleman,
who announced himself as the Reverend Robert Herrick,
came to me with a letter of introduction from Mr Keats,
my friend and fellow-poet. Mr Herrick was suffering from
an unhappy love-affair, being in alternate moods of ecstasy
and despair over a lady of the name of Julia: and it was the
hope of Mr Keats that our lakeland air and the grandeur
of our mountains would combine to restore him to a more
independent outlook. With this end in view I suggested an
excursion to the Loughrigg Fells, Mr Southey being our
companion on the journey. Unfortunately Nature was
hindered in her restorative work by one of those seasonal
mists which shrouded her beauties; and though I kept our
guest in touch with the different features of interest which
he would have seen had they been visible, he continued in a
state of dejection. In the endeavour to rouse him from this
mood I declaimed some of the nobler and more elevating
lines from such poems as I had then written or was contemplating. Barely had I uttered the first line before he burst out
with some wild reference to Julia, the young woman of
whom he was enamoured. Again and again I attempted with
some new passage to calm him, and again and again, with
some rhapsody or complaint about Julia, he would interrupt
me. Finally I desisted. At this point there came into my mind
a walk with my friend Mr Jones, when he was experiencing
a similar emotional disturbance. But how differently he had
responded to the comfort which I had essayed to give him!
Immediately the first line of the sonnet which follows leapt
into my consciousness, and before our excursion was over the

whole composition had assumed its present shape. I might add that my friend Mr Macbean of Glasgow, to whom I sent a copy, considered it to be one of the finest of my sonnets, and frequently said so to my Sister.

3. *Further Remarks by Harold Appleby-Dodds, Esq., Author of 'Wordsworthiana', 'Southeyana', 'Coleridgiana', &c.*

The reader can imagine with what eagerness I turned to the second page of the manuscript, hoping to share the felicity of Mr Macbean. He can imagine also with what astonishment my eyes encountered, not a noble sonnet of fourteen lines beginning 'Jones! when I walked with you and Wilkinson', but a poem of three 8-line verses, which had no connexion whatever either with Mr Jones *or* Mr Wilkinson! Moreover, it was clear that Wordsworth could not possibly be held responsible for more than half the lines.

What was the explanation?

My first thought was that Southey, obscured by the mist from the observation of his companions, had jotted down so much of their conversation, if such it can be called, as came to him; and that in some way this record had taken the place of the sonnet. But in that case where was the sonnet, and why was it not included in the poet's published works? A hasty visit to Glasgow, in the hope that some surviving member of the Macbean family might have the precious copy in his possession, proved abortive; partly owing to the abnormal number of Macbeans available, and partly owing to the difficulty in many cases of reconciling their mode of speech with the language in which I had supposed that we were conversing.

But on giving the manuscript a renewed consideration I came to a different conclusion. There was no lost masterpiece

of Wordsworth's, because Wordsworth had not only not
written the sonnet implied, but had not even written the
introduction! The whole MS., it was now clear to me, was
a *jeu d'esprit* of Southey's in mischievous mood. He had heard
Wordsworth and Herrick declaiming against each other, and
had amused himself later by making an imaginary poetic version of the encounter, prefacing it with an introduction such
as Wordsworth might have written to an imaginary sonnet.
As will be seen, the two poets speak in alternate lines. It is not,
of course, suggested that the antiphonic poet (if I may call
him so) was the Rev. Robert Herrick who wrote *Hesperides*.
The author of those sprightly poems was born in 1591, and
even if the announcement of his death in 1674 had been pre-
mature, he would have been 228 years old at this time, and
in no condition either for climbing fells or (one hopes) in-
dulging in amorous speculations. But the visitor to Rydal
was almost certainly a descendant of the older poet; and by a
pleasant, if uncritical, exercise of the imagination, we may
titillate ourselves with the whimsical fancy that the Julia here
referred to was herself descended from the Julia who figures
so largely in the *Hesperides*.

Here, then, is the second page of the manuscript.

4. *The Second Page.*

> The world is too much with us; late and soon
> *I think of Julia, and am like to swoon.*
> How sweet it is, when mother Fancy mocks,
> *To picture Julia tying up her locks;*
> Earth has not anything to show more fair
> *Than is the ribbon in my Julia's hair.*
> Dull would he be of soul who could pass by
> *The light that beckons from my Julia's eye.*

It is a beauteous evening, calm and free.
I wait for Julia 'neath my almond tree,
Breathless with adoration; the broad sun
Will find my waiting hardly yet begun.
Getting and spending we lay waste our powers—
Sometimes I wait for hours and hours and hours:
Thoughts that do often lie too deep for tears
Have made it seem like years and years and years.

Once did she hold the gorgeous East in fee,
Submissive to her will, and now holds me.
(A noticeable man with large grey eyes
Was Henry East, and famous for his ties).
We have given our hearts away, a sordid boon,
To one as fickle as th' inconstant moon.
Milton! thou shouldst be living at this hour,
Thy Paradise Regained in Julia's bower!

5. *Final Statement by Harold Appleby-Dodds, Esq., Author of* 'Whither Wordsworth?', 'Wordsworth: Whither?' &c.

It only remains to add that Southey's sense of mischief had prompted him to a further irreverence, mercifully not carried beyond the opening couplet. It will be remembered that Mr Herrick came to Rydal with an introduction from Keats. Southey, we must suppose, had wickedly imagined an encounter in the neighbourhood of Hampstead similar to the one overheard by him on the Loughrigg Fells. On the back of the poem given above he had written:

I stood tip-toe upon a little hill,
And got my chin on Julia's window-sill——

Fortunately he realized in time that this was hardly a posture for a beneficed clergyman, and pressed the matter no further.

I may perhaps be forgiven for intruding my private affairs

upon the notice of the reader so far as to say that I have just
added a codicil to my will, bequeathing the MS. of Southey's
jeu d'esprit to the British Museum.

Such is Mr Appleby-Dodds' story. It only remains to add
that, in sending it to me for publication, he was good enough
to let me study the original documents here described. It was
evident that two words in the fourth line of the poem had
been corrected, the original version of them being still just
decipherable. As first conceived, then, the third and fourth
lines would have run:

> How sweet it is when mother Fancy mocks
> To picture Julia pulling up her socks.

Whether the poet pictured the lady as engaged literally or
figuratively in the exercise mentioned is not clear, but in
either case it would seem that a more modern voice than
Southey's is speaking to us. I say no more. It is for the British
Museum to judge.

THE Flat Racing season opens this month, and, from all I hear, there are many people in England who are more interested in it than I am. Possibly if I had ever won as much as sixpence by, with, from or on a horse, my enthusiasm for the sport might be as great as theirs. The nearest I ever got to improving the breed of horses was when I drew an animal called Bachelor's Wedding in a Derby sweepstake, and got married on the day of the race. If ever a horse had encouragement to win, then that horse did. From all I read of form, a horse called Bachelor's Wedding, running in the Derby on a day when a bachelor who is interested in him is actually getting wedded, stands at least as much chance as a horse whose great-aunt on his mother's side won over the distance at Pontefract five years ago. Whether those chances are improved if he goes to the post 'sweating slightly' I have never discovered. This is one of the things about perspiration which I don't know. Let us turn our attention instead to another problem which must often have puzzled the Jockey Club, though naturally it has been too proud to say so. Here it is:

Why should a horse in a race for two-year-olds be entered as Queen of the Sahara colt or Beatrice filly, and not, as most of the others are, as Kiss Me Quick?

I have given a good deal of thought to this subject, upon

which so much of our export drive depends, and I am now in a position to offer the only five possible solutions of the problem. None of them is completely convincing, but obviously one of them must be correct.

1. Beatrice, who is in an interesting condition, is about to have a small horse. Owing to a hiatus in medical science nobody knows whether it is to be a boy or a girl. It is obviously impossible, therefore, to decide its name in advance, for this might lead to the gross impropriety of calling a colt Gertrude. As soon as the little one is born, and its sex ascertained, a telegram is sent to the Clerk of the Course at Gatfield, entering 'Beatrice colt' for the Upper Swampington Two-Year-Old Stakes in two years' time. This must be done *without delay*, otherwise your horse may be seven years old before there is a vacancy, and somebody will notice this. The telegram sent, then and *only then* you have leisure to think of a name. You decide on Archibald, and send another telegram beginning '*Re* my earlier telegram'. Well, you know what happens when you start doing that sort of thing. The Clerk of the Course flips over a few old telegrams, says, 'Oh, demmit, I can't be bothered now,' and goes out to lunch. And, to your surprise, Archibald strips for his first race as 'Beatrice colt'.

(*Objection.*—Why doesn't the owner think of alternative names beforehand? *Answer.*—The more alert-minded do, but the standard isn't very high.)

2. Beatrice has twins. You are very quick off the mark this time, and call them James and John as soon as you know. Then you prepare (obtain telegraph form, sharpen pencil, etc.) to enter one of them for the T.Y.O. Stakes—but *which*? It may be John who turns out to be the race-horse and James the cab-horse, *or the other way round*. So you just say 'Beatrice

colt', and give them a lot of gallops against each other, leaving the decision until the day of the race; so that, even if you had decided on John months before, and he suddenly goes down with a nasty cold, you can still whizz in James.

(*Objection*.—Horses don't have twins. *Answer*.—Beatrice was a mare.)

3. You just can't think of a name before the Swampington Stakes are run. Yes, I know, you ought to be able to in two years, but you can't. You try and try. Probably what it comes to is that your wife wants to call it Queen Rose of the Rosebud Garden of Girls, but you say it's much too long, and you want to call it Maisie, but your wife says (among other things) that her legs were much too short, because you once knew a little girl called Maisie, though there was absolutely nothing in it, just both liking Edgar Wallace, but in the idiotic way women have, your wife—well, anyhow, you offer to split the difference and call it Edna, which was another girl you knew, and she offers to compromise with Scarlett O'Hara, and after a lot more argument you have to have another compromise . . . and so it goes on. When the race is run, it still hasn't got a name, or rather it has two names, because you always call it Maisie, and she always calls it Hilary, a frightful twerp in the jute business you thought she'd forgotten, and as you can't have a horse with two names because of upsetting the bookmakers, it has to run as 'Beatrice filly'.

(*Objection*.—Why did he marry her? *Answer*.—You may well ask.)

4. You are doing all this in a sordid way for money. Beatrice's little boy-horse had been following you about for two years, with a pleading look in its big brown eyes, saying, 'Keep me! Don't send me away to strangers!' But that is

just what you are going to do—you cad. As soon as it has won (or lost) the U.S. Stakes, you are going to sell it for filthy lucre. And then what? Suppose you have called it Trumpington, and it was Sir John Trumpington-Trumpington who blackballed the new owner for the Epsom Public Baths; suppose its name is Bob, and everybody in the new owner's stable, including the new owner, is called Bob; suppose its name is Easy Come, Easy Go, which was the name of his play which was such a ghastly failure; whatever you call your horse, the new owner may not like it. So you sell it as 'Beatrice colt'; and as soon as the cheque is safely through the bank, the new owner, who has *always* wanted a horse called Sonny, calls it Sonny.

(*Objection.*—He could change the name. *Answer.*—Then it mightn't come when he whistled.)

5. You are determined, whatever its sex, to call the little stranger Jujube. It is by Sucker out of Hebrew Melody, and anyway you like jujubes. To your intense chagrin you hear that there *is* a horse called Jujube, which came in last by a neck in the Middleton Plate two seasons ago. So you just have to wait till it dies, calling your own little horse 'Hi!' in the meantime (so as not to confuse it later on) and entering it as 'Beatrice colt'. For some reason which I cannot explain the early Jujube always dies before 'Beatrice colt' is a three-year-old, thus allowing Jujube (junior) to win the Derby in its own name, like a gentleman.

(*Objection.*—He could call it Jujube II. *Answer.*—This would give a sensitive horse an inferiority complex.)

So much for that.

It would be a great convenience to critics if an author's pedigree were as convincing to them as a horse's is to Our

Racing Correspondent. Having arrived in time for the end of the First Act, and having seen most of the Second, a dramatic critic could return to the bar, assured that there was no need to witness the finish, the author's uncle having had his only play hissed off the stage half-way through, and his grandmother having failed to stay the distance when dramatizing *The Pilgrim's Progress* for the village Choral Society. A literary critic could fall back upon those comparative assessments which are so popular in the stable: pointing out that as Brown had been beaten up in the Manchester (Guardian) Handicap, but not so badly as Smith who hadn't been placed among the first three Book Society's choices, then, taking a line through these two, Jones, the winner of the Hawthornden Stakes, could (but probably wouldn't) give ten pounds to either of them.

But then, as may have been observed before, horses are very different from men. When Carroway Seed has let down his great-aunt, and ignored all the comparative lines drawn up for his guidance, how often our Racing Expert will tell us, in apology, that he must have been feeling the effects of his race a fortnight ago. Small comfort this to the thousands who have lost their five shillings, and think nothing of racing to catch their trains six days a week. One feels vaguely that, if one were a race-horse, one would like racing, being the only thing that one could do; and that, the more of it one did, the better one would become. One feels, stupidly, that if one were going in for the Derby, one would like to have run a mile and a half just once, to see what it felt like, rather than to rely on the knowledge that one's father had. But no; one might suffer from the effects later. Sometimes I think that there should be a Society for the Prevention of Kindness to Animals. In the days when horses did all the work on the roads I have seen a cart-horse pulling with difficulty a heavy load up a hill, and heard sympathetic murmurs of, 'Poor thing! What a shame!' and suggestions that the cruel driver should be reported to the S.P.C.A. Why is it pitiable to be forced to exert your full strength occasionally? Nobody says 'Poor things!' at Henley.

As is now clear, I do not know very much about horses. We were London children, whose only sustained experience of country life was in the summer holidays. But in the days of our childhood a penny 'bus to the Crown, Cricklewood, would take us into the fields; and when the eldest of us was recovering from scarlet fever, it was to a farm at Hendon that he was sent. We, his younger brothers, visited him there, met real cows on terms of mutual good will, played in the hay, and wished that we could get scarlet fever too. This Hendon farm remains in my memory as the most complete realization of all that the books had said about the country. It seemed in some way more remote from London than anything which we experienced in our August migrations.

These migrations were usually to the home counties, but the first of them, when I was an unconsulted two, was to Shropshire. There is a legend, in which my faith has grown with each succeeding year, that while there I took part in a family ascent of the Wrekin; from whose crest the dawning of a new day could (it was supposed) most rapturously be heralded. Even now I can form an authentic picture of my share in the expedition; it is as much a part of my memory, which means of myself, as the hat I bought yesterday. There I am, trotting along—a little behind the others, of course, but definitely not being carried; just taking the hand of one of the laggards—and there, stretching in front of us, is the long, gentle slope to the summit. I do not claim to remember the actual dawn: that 'august sunrise', as Tennyson called it, foregoing the capital letter: though no doubt it was there as usual; and it is this reticence which makes me feel that my memory, as far as it goes, can be trusted. Naturally I have taken up rather a condescending attitude to the Wrekin ever since, regarding it as a slight distension of Nature in the Primrose Hill class; something which one strolls up after ringing the bell for breakfast, in order to see what the weather is going to be like. Having now consulted an encyclopaedia, I discover that it is in fact 'an isolated, sugar-loaf hill of 1,335 feet'. This shakes me a little. Could I at the tender age of two have walked up an isolated sugar-loaf of 1,335 feet in time to see the sun rise? Perhaps the encyclopaedia is wrong. Perhaps it is only 1,334 feet.

Not only were we as a family always ready on the tops of mountains to welcome the sun, to the moon also we gave our patronage. I have an unshakable London memory of being whisked out of sleep at some hour of which I had never heard, wrapped in an eiderdown, and carried by my father to the landing window (bordered by coloured glass) to attend a total eclipse of the moon. This was one of those failures in community of idea which are so frequent between parent and child. A rigidity in my bedtime arrangements had given me as yet little acquaintance with the moon; for when I had been up late enough to encounter it, as often as not, and for reasons never properly explained to me, it was somewhere else. Indeed, this may have been the first occasion

on which we were to come face to face; possibly I went to
bed that night singing happily to myself 'I'm going to see
the moon! I'm going to see the moon!'; so that now not to
see it, and to be told that that was the whole point, was to
strain too far a child's faith in the wonders of the Universe.

I do not blame my father for this. Any of us whose
astronomical creed has been built up on repeated assertions
of the invisibility of anything at Greenwich must feel an
expectant thrill when he reads at last that something is going
to be visible in St John's Wood; must resolve, misprint or
no misprint, to share that expectation with the family. For
who could say when it would happen again, or how long
any of us would live? Here was an experience for his children
which they would never forget . . . and, as you see, I have
never forgotten it.

Perhaps it was this early acquaintance with the dawn on
the topmost peaks of the Wrekin which decided me in my
middle-age to have a sundial.

The charm of a sundial to many people is that it enables
them to set their watches right by the sun; but to me it is
charming because it brings assurance that the sun is keeping
right by my watch. I am probably more surprised by this
perpetual rightness than is the Astronomer Royal. The fact
that the moon comes up one haberdasher's size larger night
after night gives him no thrill. He doesn't seem to fear that
something might have happened to it on the other side of
the world. I take my eye off the sun for hours, sometimes
weeks, at a time, and it turns up again just as advertised.
Einstein knows it will; Eddington knew it would; but I
have never felt quite certain. A visit to the sundial not only
reassures me, but, so to speak, puts me right with the Huxley

family. Now we all know. It is sad to think that next month our sundial will be an hour slow, and that there is no way of 'putting it on'.

There are two official mottoes for sundials. One of them says in extremely old English:

> Between ye showeres
> I mark ye houres,

and the other, in still older Latin:

> Horas non numero nisi serenas,

which is the same idea. This is like calling your house The Laburnums because it has two laburnum trees, or (*lucus a non lucendo*) because it hasn't. One prefers to be original; particularly if one is a writer by profession, daily confronted by a blank space which calls for words. Obviously one must experiment on paper first.

> There's room here for a little rhyme,
> And I'm the man to fill it:
> The sun can tell us all the time,
> But in the summer, Willett?

Humour. Perhaps, though, it is a mistake to be humorous in stone; humour favours a more temporal medium. Stone, as Moses knew, is for the moralist. What about this?

> No need to listen for the chime,
> No need to wind the clocks up;
> The sun records the fleeting time—
> Make haste, and pull your socks up.

Still a little on the light side, perhaps. Moreover, one mustn't forget that a sundial stands in a garden, and that a garden demands constant toil and attention from others. Just a hint, perhaps—

> Here stands the time
>   (Till Time itself has effaced it).
> Please note that I'm
>   The only man who may waste it.

One glance at this would send the gardener hurrying back to his hoe. Yet perhaps it is a little magisterial. This might be better:

> Whatever hour the sun may say,
>   It's always time for weeding;
> The dandelion which blooms today
>   Tomorrow will be seeding.

This may be taken literally or symbolically, as the visitor prefers. Perhaps he would do well to take it both ways: literally on reading it *in situ* and noting the trowel and fork laid carefully at the base, symbolically on thinking it over in his own home, where it doesn't matter so much, but may make things pleasanter for his family.

For my last attempt I think I shall become instructive, if slightly technical. For where so fitly as on a sundial can it be insisted that it is really our planet, not the sun, which is doing all the work? Even now, I meet men and women who give me the impression that they don't believe it. They still talk about the sun rising and setting, which is ridiculous language to use of a stationary object. Rising (particularly in the early morning, which is when the sun is alleged to do it) demands violent movement. Surely they have deceived themselves about this: surely a sundial, without some such words as these that follow, will mislead them still further.

> How slowly we absorb it,
>   When told by Men Who Know,
> That Earth maintains an Orbit
>   And *not* a Status Quo.

Yet, though the words are cryptic,
  The sentiment is true:
To orbits so elliptic
  The Flight of Time is due.

The Rich Man at his boar's head,
  The Poor Man at his bun,
Observe the flight aforesaid
  But blame it on the Sun.

I think now that I should have ordered five sundials. *Littera scripta manet*—so much more certainly on stone.

One cannot think of the sun without thinking of Joshua.

Then spoke Joshua to the Lord in the day when the Lord delivered up the Amorites before the children of Israel, and he said in the sight of Israel, 'Sun, stand thou still upon Gibeon . . .' And the sun stood still and the moon stayed until the people had avenged themselves upon their enemies. Is not this written in the book of Jasher? So the sun stood still in the midst of heaven, and hasted not to go down about a whole day. And there was no day like that before it or after it.

Certainly not after it; for if the sun suddenly 'stood still' in relation to the earth, then (as we know now, and as Jasher didn't know) this planet suddenly stopped revolving. As it was revolving at anything up to a thousand miles an hour, the result would have been complete disintegration. We may conclude, then, that this well-known passage in the Old Testament records something which did not happen;

or, at least, something which did not happen as the chronicler
supposed it to have happened.

Now it is customary to say of so much of the Old Testament as appears to be factually untrue that it was meant
symbolically only; or was just a picturesque over-statement,
common in the East, but not unknown in the West—as,
for instance, in the signing of a letter 'Your obedient servant'.
Jasher (if he is responsible) was merely saying in a picturesque
way that it was an unusually bright evening, and that the
children of Israel were thus able to go on killing the children
of the Amorites until long after sunset. But this is to interpret
Jasher in the light of knowledge which he lacked. He was
recording a legend of the Battle of Avalon which he had
heard; the story of a perfectly simple interference with the
laws of Nature, by a Deity who had often so interfered in
order to aid His chosen people. Why should he not believe
it? Everyone knew that the earth was motionless. Anyone
could see how slowly the sun moved. How little it was to
ask of Jehovah that He should raise His hand, and stay the
sun's slow course until His people's enemy was defeated. A
'miracle', yes, but such a simple one; a 'war story', but so
readily believed.

It may be said that if Jehovah could hold the sun up, he
could equally easily, and without disaster, stop the earth
revolving. True. Once you believe that an omnipotent Deity
is interfering in the Laws of Nature which He has ordained,
then any miracle is possible at any time, and none more nor
less credible than the next. Was the world made in seven
days? The geologist says no. The Churchman, not liking to
ignore geology altogether, explains that 'seven days' is sym-
bolical or picturesque or mistranslated. But it is no more
difficult to make a world in seven days than in seven million

years; and, having made it in seven days, no more difficult than either to give it the appearance of a seven-million-year-old world to a geologist. Accept Divine interference in natural laws, and you can believe anything. But to believe anything is to believe nothing.

The schoolboy defined faith as 'believing what you know isn't true'. We might call it 'belief unsupported by reason'. In the Previous Examination at Cambridge fifty years ago one was offered the choice between a paper on Paley's *Evidences of Christianity* and one on Jevons' *Elementary Logic*; which looked a little as if one were being invited at that early stage of life to decide whether faith or reason was the surer guide. I chose reason; probably for no better reason than that I was a Nonconformist and suspected that Paley wasn't. But I still trust to reason as a surer guide than somebody else's faith. A Christian, Mohammedan or Jew has a perfect right to pity those who do not share the mystical interpretation of life which brings him such comfort and such happiness, but none to condemn them for following reason where revelation has been denied. And if 'evidences' of a religion are valid, then evidence against a religion is also valid.

So, without more ado, I shall ask why Christians still accept the Old Testament as part of their Faith, when their Master gave them a New Testament. 'Idolatry', said William Temple, 'consists in worshipping God under any other conception of him than that which is set before us in the Gospels.' Why, then, do they still identify the God of Moses with the God of Jesus? The one said, 'I am a jealous God and visit the sins of the fathers upon the children unto the third and fourth generation.' And the other said, 'Suffer little children to come unto me.' Is it the same promise? 'Eye for eye, tooth for tooth, hand for hand, foot for foot,' said the God of

Moses. 'But *I* say unto you, whosoever shall smite thee on the right cheek, turn to him the other also.' Is it possible to believe both, to obey both? The Old Testament expounds the religion of the Jews; in Leviticus with great particularity. Are Christians Jews? If not, why is the Old Testament part of the Christian religion? And if it is right that it should be, why are the commands of Leviticus ignored?

The Old Testament is responsible for more atheism, agnosticism, disbelief—call it what you will—than any book ever written; it has emptied more churches than all the counter-attractions of cinema, motor-bicycle and golf course. There is much in the Gospels which needs to be explained, but nothing which needs to be explained away; much which is difficult to believe, but nothing which one would be sorry to believe.

And Jesus said Suffer the little children to come unto me, for of such is the Kingdom of God.

And as he was going up by the way, there came forth little children out of the city and mocked him. And he turned back and looked on them, and cursed them in the name of the Lord. And there came forth two she-bears out of the wood, and tare forty-and-two children of them.

How gladly, how helpfully, will the Vicar in his pulpit explain the first text. How apologetically, how feebly, will he explain away the other. And when he has explained it away, will the congregation be nearer to God?

But though the Old Testament is no part of the Christian religion, it has three values for us all. First, it has been translated into incomparable English. That seems much to me. 'I am convinced more and more day by day', said Keats, 'that fine writing is next to fine doing'; and by one quotation from Joshua I have given this book a touch of fine writing which no indistinction of mine can take away. Secondly, it establishes in history and in legend the background of the actors in the New Testament. Thirdly, and most importantly, it reveals the inspired magnanimity and audacity of Jesus, by showing us just what weight of ugly tradition he fought and conquered; just what ignoble travesty of God underlay his own transcendent vision.

Ye have heard that it was said by them of old time . . . but I say unto you——

To which voice shall we listen?

Perhaps it would be as well to explain here what I mean by the word 'million'. I used it in the last section, and shall be using it again; and I don't want the well-informed to write and tell me that my figures are inaccurate. When in 1942 Eddington sent me his book *The Philosophy of Physical Science*, he wrote:

I regret to say that on page 170 I have made a mistake of nearly four million million million million million million million million million million million million million. If you have an American visitor who brags too much about the bigness of things over there, just fish out this book and say, 'Here is an English book which contains the biggest mistake ever made!' I do not think he will be able to produce anything from his side to beat it.

You will agree with me that one would have had an equally strong feeling that a mistake had been made, if Eddington had left out two or three of those millions in his

confession. In one of the most lovely passages in the Old
Testament it is written:

And Jacob served seven years for Rachel; and they seemed
unto him but a few days for the love he had to her.

To be completely commonplace I am going to say now
that 1,000 million years seem to me but a million years for
the dislike I have of these enormous numbers. So I adopt
Humpty Dumpty's masterful attitude to the word 'million'.
It means what I want it to mean: which is 'seven figures and
as many more noughts as you like'.

All this is preliminary to some talk of the Universe. I
think that we are inclined to forget the Universe when we
make our Guesses at Truth. Lately an American clergyman
preached a sermon which was reprinted as a pamphlet, a copy
of it being sent, for some reason, to me. He was answering
the many who believe that there is no immortality save in
this world: the immortality which is Shakespeare's. However
humble, we have given something of ourselves to the future,
shall leave something of ourselves behind; and the world
will be, by that little, changed for our passing. He did not
condemn this belief as 'irreligious', that stupid word; he
considered it reasonably and sympathetically. I felt that, in
the highest sense of the adjective, he was a good man. But
his argument was this:

Scientists tell us that the world is slowly freezing up; that
in a million years from now it will be uninhabitable. If so,
and if there is no life of the spirit after death, then there is
no immortality of any kind, not even the immortality which
is Shakespeare's. In that case God has created a 'dead end',
and the whole of Creation has gone for nothing. Could anyone believe that the whole tremendous act of Creation was
meant to lead to a dead end?

This was all very well as far as it went; but—he forgot the Universe. God has created a million other worlds. Scientists may say that no life on them is possible. In that case God has created a million 'dead ends'. Why not a million and one? And if the scientists are wrong, and there is life in but one other, then the whole of Creation has *not* gone for nothing.

For we can go further than this. When scientists say that no life is possible on Mars, presumably they mean that no life is possible now. Looking at Earth a million years ago, scientists on Mars could have dismissed scornfully the idea of an earthly life; 'life', they would have added complacently, 'as *we* know it'. Can we say definitely of any heavenly body that, even if it cannot support life now, it could not have supported it a million years ago, or will not support it a million years hence? Can we say definitely that in a million years from now the last survivors of Earth will not have learnt how to fly to the nearest inhabitable star . . . taking Shakespeare with them?

I have my own theory about immortality which I give for what little it may be worth. If Man evolved from lower forms of life (as I believe), at what stage did he qualify for immortality? The qualification cannot be in time, for evolution does not go upwards in a straight line, but upwards in zig-zags; and to rule a line at any point in time would be to leave many of the fit on the wrong side of the line, and many of the unfit on the right side. Each man, then, must qualify himself. How? Being unable to imagine a fleshly body which is immortal in a world of such hazards as this, but being able to imagine an immortal spirit, I can only give myself the answer that the qualification comes when Man, on this earth, is able to give a separate life to the spirit, so that it depends no longer on the body for its support. They say that already a Yogi can do this for a few hours at a time. Then he will have those few hours of life after death. As the million years flow on, more and more people will be able to do it for longer and longer . . . and perhaps in another million years bodies will have fallen into disuse, as one small part of them has fallen even now—the appendix. We shall have evolved our immortality, as we have evolved our upright position, our capacity for reason, our appreciation of beauty and our sense of humour.

Well, that is the theory. It will appeal to nobody with whose wishful thinking it does not coincide. It will appeal to nobody who regards this world as but a noviciate for the next. It will appeal to nobody who believes that, starting from the lowest forms of life all those million years ago, evolution has reached its triumphal summit in himself, and can go no further. But it does appeal to me; because I believe that a world which reveals new wonders every day has yet to reveal something more wonderful than myself; more wonderful even than Shakespeare. Think of it: we press a button, and magically there comes over the air to us from 10,000 miles away the voice of a man who died ten years ago. A wonderful invention of our scientists, we say. Yes, but they did not invent it, they only discovered it. It was invented by God. His invention has been there for a million years, waiting to be discovered. In another million years we shall have discovered many other things. We have still a long way to go before we have discovered everything.

Any mention of 'religion' in public, unless by one suitably frocked, will lead to a protest from somebody. 'It isn't a thing one talks about, and certainly not in the same breath—well, chapter, then—as ridiculous nonsense about racehorses. Anyway, what do *you* know about it?' And so on. Well, I don't know that I know very much about anything; but, if alive, one must think, and, if a writer, must write. It would be silly to say 'I musn't think about God now, because I've just been thinking about the Derby. Better wait till Sunday.' And it would be still more silly to say 'I mustn't think about God at all, because I don't know anything about Him. I must wait for somebody to tell me.'

Waiting to be told what you believe is good sense in Russia. It would have been good sense in England a few hundred years ago. But, thank God, it is not good sense in England today.

APRIL

THERE are three of us who make the garden what it is (or, as we tell ourselves when it isn't, what it will be); my wife, our gardener and myself.

I put Her first, because it is really Her garden. She never stops planning for it, brooding over it, working in it. When she is in the bathroom after a morning's weeding, doing what she can for herself with a slice of lemon, she is still thinking about it. She takes catalogues to bed with her. Without Her there would be no garden.

Modestly I put our Gardener second.

Gardeners can be divided into two classes: those whose life is centred in the kitchen-garden—and ours. Ours is the only gardener who would rather grow salvia than celery. For this we treasure him. Vegetables are no satisfaction to the owner until they arrive on the table. If one can buy a carrot, then one will get all from a carrot which a carrot can give. It is a short-lived pleasure at best, and then only for those who like carrots. But flowers give a prolonged delight to all, both in the garden and out of it; and though one can buy cut flowers, one cannot buy the happiness which they give as they grow.

I have said that our gardener would rather grow salvia

than celery, and this is true; but though he is friendly with salvia, and particularly salvia Turkestan, he is an extravagant mother to dahlias and chrysanthemums. They make up the greater part of his life. All through the year he is propagating and nursing chrysanthemums; against the great day in November when he staggers down to the house with pot after pot, and masses them along the end wall of the sitting-room. By April he has dug in most of his dahlias. This is as well, for the garden lies low, and an early September frost will kill them in a night. Last year Lady Aileen was flowering in June, which gave him nearly four months in which to dote on her. In the dahlia world this is a long life for a mother.

The third member of the partnership is myself. I provide (among other things) what is so necessary if beauty is to prosper: admiration.

Nobody could feel more grateful to his partners than I: a gratitude frequently expressed (once a week in the case of the Second Gardener), and always in my heart. But it is not to them that I owe my more personal pleasure.

There was a scene in an early play of Somerset Maugham's in which a well-preserved woman discouraged a callow and rather troublesome admirer by admitting him to the intimacy of her dressing-table at the moment when she was making up her face; this, you understand, was before the happy days when the privilege was graciously extended to the general public. I cannot help feeling that my two partners must know something of that young man's disillusion. Attending the accouchement of one's favourite chrysanthemum, or powdering one's rose with what I used to think was horse-and-hound but now know to be hoof-and-horn, may be interesting work in itself, but subtracts something, surely, from the pleasurable surprise of the result. They know what to expect, and at the best it does, and at the worst it doesn't, fulfil their expectations.

Something of the certainty, and inevitably of the disappointment, is handed on to me. If no slugs, moles or late frosts intervene, the work of my partners will be beautiful, but not wholly unimagined. What I most love in our garden are the little bits in the picture which Nature puts in for herself; sometimes with broad careless sweeps of the brush, sometimes with the particularity of the fastidious artist, just here, just there. In short, I love the flowers which come Heaven knows how from Heaven knows where.

I do not think that we have sown, pricked out, planted or had any formal dealings with agrostemma or eschscholtzia for twenty-five years. Yet year after year agrostemma (Ladies Pricknose, as it is more beautifully called) flits across the garden and establishes herself in some bed or wall far distant from her girlish home. However lovingly a corner is redesigned by one of my partners for blue flowers only, and however laboriously redug by the other, golden eschscholtzia will still blow its independent trumpet. Aubrietia—well, one looks for independence from aubrietia. But how cunningly it will plant itself in crevices where the hand of man cannot go; will even (it seems) bring its own earth with it, and make a home for itself on barren steps.

This I love. A cynic might say that my love is no more than delight in an unearned, unexpected bonus. This is entirely to misjudge me. It comes from a feeling, which grows on me with the years, that since my partners can claim their own share in the monthly income of beauty earned by their labours, this unclaimed, unworked-for bounty is in some mysterious way the product of my own idleness. It is I who am responsible for it.

Holding myself thus responsible, naturally I take an artist's pride in my effects. One of my most charming is the way I colour wild primroses; sometimes, even, with the aid of a casual cowslip, turning them into polyanthus. A visitor, coming across them in a wall or a crack of paving, or, perhaps more surprisingly, among a sheet of primroses in the wood, will cry, 'Oh, look at that! Isn't that sweet?' and I admit it modestly. But if she asks, 'However do you manage it?' I say that it is a trade secret. In fact, it would be difficult to explain. Had either of my two partners been responsible, it would have been cross-fertilization, or something equally boring. With me it was just a careless thought. 'Why not?' I said.

Perhaps this is why the rose, which is so many people's favourite flower, has never been mine. I can do nothing with roses. No rose has ever seeded itself; or, if it has, its birth pangs have returned it to briar. Among the other flowers I have my ups and downs. I can do more with lupins (though not with such lovely varieties as Heather Glow and George Russell) than I can do with delphiniums. In fact, I don't think that I have ever achieved an accidental delphinium, but I am still trying, for I love it dearly. Coreopsis is child's play to me. It comes up in the paving wherever I snap my fingers. Sidalcea is becoming a habit; indeed, there are times when I fear that I am getting carried away. This goes also for myosotis (to give it its grander name), though every now and then I achieve a pink variety which is generally esteemed. Sweet William has eluded me so far, but I am still hoping.

Before we leave the garden for the wood I must say something about thrift; not the 'Thrift, thrift, Horatio' of which Hamlet spoke, but *armeria plumbagineae*. This, as anyone who has read a garden book knows, is 'an excellent plant for forming an evergreen grass-like edging to flower-borders. Most kinds flourish in ordinary soil and may be increased by dividing the tufts in spring or early autumn'. What it comes to is this. You plant a piece of thrift the size of a pin-cushion, and in two years it is the size of a hassock. You divide the hassock into twenty pieces the size of a pin-cushion, each of which in two years is the size of a hassock, which is divided into twenty pieces the size of a pin-cushion, each of which in two years . . . but I need not go on. One's motto is clearly 'The more, the armeria'. In ten years nothing but thrift is visible as far as the eye can reach. So far from having an evergreen grass-like edging to flower-borders, the best one can hope for is an occasional flower edging to an evergreen grass-like border, an evergreen grass-like croquet lawn, and an evergreen grass-like summer-house.

When I realized what was happening, I announced my intention of abandoning thrift—much to the relief of the First Gardener, who was studying bulb catalogues. In any case it was becoming too much like work.

We planted the wood, tree by tree. By 'we' I mean that twenty years ago it was a thistly field; and when the donkey died, we engaged a man to engage a posse of men to turn it into a wood. We ourselves, however, even I, helped to fill it with daffodils, bluebells and primroses, so that it is now as much like a wood as any other wood, only more exciting. One of the lessons which you learn in the country is never to put off doing a thing because you will be dead before you can enjoy it. If you do, you will find that ten years later you are saying 'If *only* we had planted that wistaria (peach tree, yew hedge, lime avenue) when first we talked about it!'— and you are filled with sad thoughts, like Whittier, and tell yourselves that of course *now* it *is* too late. It isn't; it never is.

Do it even now, and if you don't live to enjoy it, somebody else will. So, foolish though it seemed at the time, we planted a wood, and have thanked Heaven for it ever since.

I say Heaven, because the unconsidered things which go on in the wood are on too grand a scale for me to claim them. Observe the bluebells, an army with banners, sweeping steadily over the hill, like the invading Tartars, instead of popping up and down in their own reservation, as you would expect; in a little while they will be through the lych-gate and into the garden, and who is to stop them? The wild daffodils overflow their banks year after year, and, withdrawing, leave golden pools behind them. Frankly I don't know how it is done. Birds, say some, but you cannot put it all on to birds. It would be much more sensible if you said moles.

A wood has much to offer the gardener. At school there used to be a form called the Army Class, into which retired all those promising athletes who had failed to reach the intellectual level of their age group, and were in danger of superannuation. In the Army Class there was no age limit, and there they passed the autumn of their days, concentrating on their batting averages. In the same way a shrub or flowering tree which is not holding its own in the garden can be passed into the wood, with no further obligation on either side. It may wither away, in which case it will not be missed; or in some measure recover; or even take on a new form of life, as did the dead Dorothy Walpole standard which is now a flourishing laburnum tree. Strange things can happen in a wood.

We are now back in the garden again; and before we say goodbye to it I must tell you of my one admitted (and admired) contribution to the manual work that goes on. I

have a wonderful hand with weeds. You will notice, please,
that I said hand, not trowel. Anybody can dig up a dandelion
who digs deep enough. It takes the Third Gardener to winkle
it out with a finger and thumb, and exhibit proudly to the
First Gardener an unbroken root nine inches long. I don't
do this often, because I don't like to interrupt my partners
when they are working; besides, I prefer contemplating.
But I can do it.

Between April 21 and May 20 Shakespeare, Brahms and
Edward II were born. They were all born under the sign of
Taurus, and, if they had been living at the same time, the
Sunday Astrologer would have been giving them identical
advice for the safe conduct of their affairs in the current week.
They would all have been told that they should 'go slow on
Monday', that Tuesday was the best day for 'getting ahead
with plans', that 'domestic difficulties' would arise on Wednesday, that they would make 'a good business contact' on
Thursday, and so on. This forecast would not only apply to
these three diverse characters, but to everybody, man, woman
and child, born between April 21 and May 20. The baby-in-
arms would receive a setback in business, the centenarian
would have trouble with his business colleagues. In the
peculiar world of the Sunday Astrologer, every male, from
cradle to grave, works in a business office of some sort, has
continuous ups and downs of fortune, and returns home in
the evening to a wife who is at the mercy of a similarly
planned existence. If, as is probable, she was born under a

different sign, then their days of quarrelling with each other may be different; and what they do about that I don't know.

The stupidity and impudence exhibited by the Sunday Astrologer almost take the breath away, so that one can hardly talk about him without becoming incoherent. But it should be possible to consider astrology calmly.

To the endless discussion between Free Will and Determinism Karl Pearson (deriving, possibly, from Winwood Reade) made this contribution: that the individual might have a power of choice which was denied to mankind. If you toss a penny in the air, and invite a number of people to call heads or tails, each has a free choice, and may be right or wrong; so that with three people, the rights to wrongs may be three to nothing. But with a million people guessing, the balance will be more even, and of an infinite number of guesses, half must be right and half wrong. Each person has been left a free choice, but the result was already determined. So the life of each man is in his own hands, but the future of Humanity is pre-ordained.

Possibly I have misrepresented Karl Pearson; possibly it was a well-known theory long before he was born. In any discussion about fundamentals one must expect to be told, with the patronage which serves all need of argument, that, my dear fellow, one is talking pure Whatsitism, which was 'exploded' centuries ago. In fact, no theory about the meaning and purpose of life has ever been exploded, nor ever will be, though each may have its term of favour. Whether 'Pearsonism' is old or new, false or true, it seems reasonable.

But to have free-will still leaves one within very narrow confines. Much to my regret I am not free to become a painter, even though the curriculum of the modern school makes me feel that this freedom may not long be withheld.

I doubt if I was ever free to be a singer or a high-jumper, and certainly never to be a heavyweight boxer; nor free, of course, to be a hundred other more desirable things. We are all confined to some extent by a physical and mental constitution ordained at birth, if not specifically by our Creator. Astrology confines us still more closely, though whether actively or passively, as instrument or record, is not quite clear to me.

The position of certain stars at the moment of our birth directs our lives; so that on a particular Wednesday fifty years later, the stars in their new positions will enable us to 'push ahead energetically with a big business scheme', even if we are the invalid wife of a Chinese peasant. That would be one theory. The alternative is that the stars themselves have no impetus in the matter, but merely record the destiny marked out for us by our Creator. It was decided, dear Baby, at your birth on June 25, 1950, that on April 17, 1951, 'interesting moves bringing a welcome change affecting your job' could be expected. You would have known nothing about this in the ordinary way, but, fortunately for you, the stars are there to record the decision, and so to get you in good trim for what is coming.

Now this is not only pre-determination for us, but equally for the Creator; who has either handed over our destiny to the ineluctable stars, or (which comes to the same thing from our point of view) has left the record to them, and is compelled to keep in line with it. Should He feel after a few thousand years that too many people were having the same good business contacts, and that a change was advisable, He would have to get in touch with the Sunday Astrologer, in some way not easily to be imagined. One gathers that He has not done this, and that Friday week will continue to bring trouble with business colleagues to a twelfth of the world's population.

It is the unequal distribution of talents, capacities and constitutions at birth which makes the cry of 'Fair Shares for All' so vain. No doubt the argument still seems valid to some that, if God chose to make an 'unfair' distribution of His gifts, it is an impertinence in Man to seek to improve upon Him. These are the people who believe that the rich man in his castle, the poor man at his gate, God made them high and lowly, and ordered their estate. One need not believe anything so silly to be convinced of the vanity of 'fair shares'. The machinery of Government can do no more than provide equal shares, and equal shares mean unfair shares. Bread rationing meant that half the population was denied the bread it needed, while the other half was overloaded with bread which it didn't want. Clothes rationing meant that an actor, who had not only to be well-dressed in private, but to provide his own stage clothes, was given the same facilities for buying them as the gypsy or the hermit.

No doubt some such 'fairness' is inevitable, but at times it became ridiculous. When cars could only be moved within fixed limits for fixed purposes, France offered tourists from this country an unrestricted access to petrol. Would-be travellers craved permission from Authority to overstep their boundaries for once, so that they might get their cars to Dover. They were told that it would not be 'fair' to the many who did not want to get their cars to Dover. When a countryman asked if he might keep, fatten, kill and eat a pig in a purely private way, his excuse for such an outrageous request being that he had an unlimited supply of windfall fruit, and need make no demands on the pig-meal ration, he was told that such uncivic conduct would not be 'fair' to the people who had no windfall fruit.

So with the food subsidies, which work out at 3s. 6d. per week per stomach. Nothing could be 'fairer'; nothing more admirable than the desire to keep the price of food down—even if it remained difficult to keep the food itself down. But I still don't see why Lord Nuffield should be given a weekly dole of 3s. 6d. a week; nor, indeed, why I should. And when I read, as I have read this morning, that this country spends exactly 3s. 6d. per gambler per week on Football Pools, it is difficult not to feel that what the Government is really subsidizing is betting. So much more on the price of food doesn't mean less food, it means less money spent on pools, cinemas and tobacco. Except in the case of pensioners and people who have retired on small invested savings, and who are still wondering what 'fair shares' mean, the Food Subsidies subsidize everything except food. Most of all, they subsidize a Government at election time.

This business of betting is a little puzzling to the uninterested onlooker. The result of Football Pool betting (and to a large extent of other betting) is to take a great deal of money from the many, and redistribute it among the few. The whole idea of Socialism ('fair shares for all') is to take the money from the few and redistribute it among the many. You would expect, then, that Socialists would be passionately opposed to Football Pools, and that a Socialist Government would regard the suppression of betting as its first and most obvious duty. Nohow and Contrariwise. However reprehensible it may be to profit by the chance of being a rich man's son, and so to inherit his hard-earned money, it becomes an admirable exercise in social welfare to profit by the chance of a foul in the penalty area on a particular man at a particular time, and so to receive £50,000 tax-free; the money being collected from those who can least afford to lose it. I don't disapprove of betting, any more than I disapprove of canasta and speedway racing, to mention two other pursuits which I do not follow. Let everybody enjoy himself as he prefers. Nor shall I be so fatuous as to say that there's nothing wrong with betting 'as long as you can afford it', for this applies to every other way of spending money. But I shall continue to think that it is not a very good example of Fair Shares for All.

To return to the stars. Fortunately for mankind Shakespeare refused to submit his destiny to them, and, having found his job, stuck to it, with the pleasant result that a new season is now beginning at Stratford. I ventured to say once that 'many critics write of a Shakespearian production as if the ideal *Macbeth* were waiting round the corner for the ideal producer and the ideal cast. The ideal *Macbeth* is an impossibility.' When challenged on this by John Drinkwater and others, I tried to explain what I meant. What I meant was this.

A play is not a novel. A play is not an objective work of art, but a subjective entertainment. One can write a novel and imagine nobody reading it. One cannot write a play and imagine nobody seeing it. A play infers, and demands,

an audience. It is the business of the dramatist to be aware
of the audience, as it is not the business of the novelist to be
aware of the reader. The reason why many novelists who are
great artists (Stevenson and James, for instance) have not
been great dramatists is that they have not been aware of
their audience; that is, they have written their plays as artists
only, not as craftsmen.

Why this difference between a play and a novel? Because
the theatre is an unreal place, and a play an unreal thing. We
go to a realistic play and say 'How real! How true! How
like life!' In essentials it is true, but in detail it is utterly untrue. Imagine yourself putting your head in at the window
of a strange house and listening to the conversation for three-
quarters of an hour. There would be long silences; people
would go in and out without explanation; there would be
references to unknown Johns and Marys; private, unintelligible jokes; and even if the scene suddenly became intensely dramatic the cook would spoil it by putting her head
into it, and asking (if it were a costume play) whether there
were any orders for the butcher.

Yet in the theatre you think that you are seeing real life.
Why? Because it is the dramatist's job to make you think so,
and because, in this particular case, he happens to be a good
craftsman. It isn't a dramatist's job to 'be real', but to 'seem
real'. Shakespeare said that his end was 'to hold the mirror
up to nature'. The audience looks in the mirror and sees the
reflection. Every morning I look in the mirror and see myself
shaving with the left hand. If I want to see real life in the
mirror, I have to behave unnaturally, and shave with the
wrong hand. A good craftsman makes his characters behave
unnaturally, in order that to the audience, looking in the
mirror, they shall seem natural.

A dramatist, then, has to be intensely conscious of his audience. This fact offends the highbrow, who sees in it, as he is always quick to see, a disgraceful prostitution of somebody else's art. There is no prostitution about it. If you can't put real life on the stage (as you can't), and if you must substitute a similitude of life (as you must), you have, by that, lost the artist's complete unawareness of his public; for a similitude must look like something to somebody, and that somebody has therefore to be considered. If you object to considering anybody but yourself, for fear you should lose your integrity, don't be a dramatist. And don't be an architect. Wren was a great artist, but he tried to make the inside of St. Paul's look like a cathedral to the Dean and Chapter.

A dramatist, then, writes for his audience. But what audience? Obviously the contemporary audience. A producer may give *Macbeth* an exact Elizabethan production on an exact Elizabethan stage, but one thing is certain: he cannot give the play an exact Elizabethan audience. The audience is an integral part of the setting of the play. It is absurd to suppose that when a great craftsman designs a work of art for a particular setting, it can be wrenched out of its setting, and put, without loss, into a different one.

Consider the opening of *As You Like It*.

Enter Orlando and Adam.

ORL. As I remember, Adam, it was upon this fashion bequeathed me by will but poor a thousand crowns, and, as thou sayest, charged my brother on his blessing to breed me well.

To an Elizabethan audience this would have seemed natural, and, if it had tried to look behind the mirror, ingenious. Every play (except the human comedy) starts with a situation, and the situation has to be explained; not in this case to Adam, who knew all about it, but to the audience which was eager to learn. But, since then, how many heroes have expounded the situation to how many butlers, or how many butlers to how many housemaids, or how many heroines to how many friends, on how many telephones, in how many thousand plays? Can the opening of *As You Like It* seem natural and ingenious now?

Consider Rosalind as Ganymede, or any of Shakespeare's heroines in man's dress: Viola, Julia, Portia, Nerissa. Why was this sort of masquerade so popular? Because an Elizabethan audience was as accustomed to the stage convention that young men in women's clothes were young women, as we are to the stage convention that a room has three walls only. So they accepted (conventionally and happily) Rosalind as Rosalind, and (naturally and happily) Rosalind as Ganymede. But since our conventions allow us to see actresses on the stage, we can only accept Rosalind as Rosalind. We can't believe in Ganymede, and find it difficult to believe that Orlando did.

I have given two simple examples. But it is not all as simple as this. Arnold Bennett said once that a play was a collaboration between six entities: author, manager, producer, actor, designer, audience. Shakespeare had to consider the other five: four in his case, as Burbage was probably manager and producer. We can pick out a few simple examples of how he did this, but we can be sure that we have missed many others, more delicate, more intangible.

So, then, we come to this. We read the plays of that master-artist and master-craftsman, Shakespeare, and, in reading, we enjoy the art, not the craft. The play is put on the stage, and, for all the new emotions we experience, we have an unhappy feeling that we have lost something. We call in this and that doctor: Irving, Tree, Barker, and the many more of today. In desperation we put the play into modern dress, hoping to recapture that elusive something. For a moment (for some of the audience) this almost seems to bring it back, but the illusion goes. We cannot see Shakespeare as we feel we should. And so we blame everybody; everybody but the right man, Shakespeare—the consummate craftsman who so attuned his plays to his own audiences that, played before any other, they will always be a little off the note. For his art was for all time; but his craft was only for his age.

We never knew what Mr Brown's profession was. He was a thick-set emotionless man, who might have been tax-collector or sanitary engineer, builder or undertaker; or perhaps had retired from being one of these things. He lived in an ugly little semi-detached villa a few miles away, and grew violas in his back yard. It was the sort of back yard which includes two or three caged and disillusioned ferrets and the week's washing, surroundings which seemed inappropriate for violas. Yet locally he had a name for them, and we used to drive over in April to replace the casualties of the winter. We missed one April, and when the next one came round he was not there. The strange woman who opened the door told us that Mr Brown's brother had died in Australia nearly two years ago, leaving him a large fortune. Naturally Mr Brown was now living in a much grander place a little way along. So we went a little way along too. It was a new but pleasant-looking house: what an estate agent would have called 'an attractive gentleman's residence standing in its own spacious grounds'; and the spacious grounds were now turned into a complete nursery garden in which Mr Brown grew everything. Except ferrets.

He received us with a restrained courtesy; he was still wearing his black tie. We expressed our admiration of his charming house, as pretty as a picture in its new spring finery. He thanked us gravely. His voice hushed our enthusiasm. He said reproachfully:

'I erected it as a memorial to my brother.'

Alas! there are now strangers in the memorial, and we seek our violas elsewhere.

IN the May Election of 1929 I decided to exercise in verse
my as yet unexercised talent as a political satirist. I sat down,
therefore, and pondered on what the politicians were calling
the Vital Issues Before the Country. But, being myself in the
country at the time, I could not help feeling that the only
'issues' which really mattered were the apple and cherry
blossom, the budding flowers, and the fresh pale green of
birch and beech; and, feeling this, could not but wish that my
Lords Birkenhead and Beaverbrook and other thunderous
politicians agreed with me; and could not help regretting
that the loveliness of May was lost for so many in the
clamour of a General Election. So, between the issues involved, my verses wavered for a little, and finally settled
down to this:

> The doves take up their lullabies ;
>   Reluctant clouds are newly fled;
> The sun upon the meadow lies
>   (*Said Beaverbrook to Birkenhead*).
> From elm to elm drops idly down
>   The homely chatter of the rook.

The beech is in her new green gown
  (*Said Birkenhead to Beaverbrook*).

Upon the hill the patient sheep
  Stand waiting, and the lambs are fed.
Beneath the oak the shadows creep
  (*Said Beaverbrook to Birkenhead*).
A lazy wind, which stopped to play,
  And from the alders gently shook
A whisper, smiles itself away
  (*Said Birkenhead to Beaverbrook*).

Picked out in patterns on the wall
  The apples blossom white and red,
And white and red their petals fall
  (*Said Beaverbrook to Birkenhead*).
Forget-me-nots their faith renew,
  And from forgotten crannies look,
To match the sky in matchless blue
  (*Said Birkenhead to Beaverbrook*).

Proud irises in spires of green,
  Their golden heads still covered
Unto their pale reflections lean
  (*Said Beaverbrook to Birkenhead*).
And, green and gold, new kingcups float
  Whose seeds the streams of autumn took
To make enchantment of the moat
  (*Said Birkenhead to Beaverbrook*).

Drowsed by the sun the cottage sleeps
  As afternoon and Silence wed . . .
But deeps are calling unto deeps,
  And Beaverbrook to Birkenhead.
'*For roof the sky, the earth for bed,*
  Ah, would were ours the shepherd's crook!'
Cries Frederick, Lord Birkenhead;
  Sighs Max (1st Baron Beaverbrook).

Sometimes I think that the inclusion of these two revered names has a little marred the whole as poetry, and that as political satire it was never going to be very much good.

But the wind bloweth where it listeth, and one is at the mercy of any sudden malevolent puff. I was asked to write a World Song For Girl Guides. Who better? A world song for girl guides? Of course! I sharpened a pencil, and surrendered myself to the Muse. A world . . . song . . . for . . . girl . . . guides. A song which would be sung round a hundred camp fires in a hundred lands! Wonderful to be the author of such a song! Presumably it would be translated first into the other ninety-nine languages. That was a pity; that would take something away from it. The idea, yes, but not the words, would be mine. Ah! but at a Rally in England, then, whatever the colour, race or creed of each group, they would all sing it in English! Happily I imagined them doing this . . . Perhaps it would have been better if I hadn't.

> Guides, fall in, and take your stations!
> Guides from half a hundred nations!
> (One whose name I shall not mention
> Needs to blow her nose.) *Attention!*
>
> Guides must all be neat not gaudy
> (Someone's slip is showing, Maudie).
> Stockings are the worst offenders—
> Take a pull on your suspenders.
>
> Here we stand with shining faces
> (Someone's—yes, I think it's Grace's—
> Shines perhaps a shade too brightly.
> Too late now, but cream it nightly);
>
> Here in sweet communion banded,
> Here we stand with chests expanded

(Chests, not tummies, Jane), and proudly
Sing the World Song—much too loudly.

I decided that I was rather busy just now, and that the Poet Laureate or somebody like that would probably do it better.

To write properly of asparagus (and now is the time to do it) one needs a fine feathery pen. Mine has had a hair in it for a week. Somebody ought to look into this question of superfluous hair in pens. Whence does it come, whither does it go? Or, more profitably, why does it never go? Start the morning with a hair in your pen, and there are two of you writing for the rest of the session. I apologize for my collaborator.

Asparagus. A beautiful word to which the poets have never done justice. When Longfellow wrote 'The Wreck of the Hesperus', did he never—wait a moment. Was it Longfellow who wrote 'The Wreck of the Hesperus'? I am shaky on wrecks; there are too many of them in literature.

> It was the schooner Hesperus
>   That sailed the wintry sea;
> The boy stood on its burning deck
>   Whence all had fled but he—
> 'By thy long beard and glittering eye,
>   Now wherefore stopp'st thou me?'
> Toll for the brave.

You see how easily one gets confused. Well, when Southey wrote 'The Wreck of the Hesperus', did he never stop and think to himself, 'How much better this would be if I could make it something about asparagus'? I suppose not. But

breathes there a bard with soul so dead, who *never* to himself
has said, 'If I can write of asphodel, why not asparagus as
well?' I cannot believe it. Asparagus, or the Works, Human
and Divine, of Robert Herrick.

Even our novelists have been reticent, though there may be
a reason for that. Asparagus is just a little—is it not?—obvious. We should suspect a novelist who took his heroine to
the Savoy and gave her asparagus. We should say 'This man
knows nothing of high life, and is playing for safety.' For
what we like to read about is that little dinner *à deux*, *chez*
Casani, at which, as he unfolds his napkin the hero can
remark casually to the admiring heroine, 'I always say that
Casani's is the only place in London where they know how
to do a *sole à la bonne femme.*' Then, since he is 'one of the few
men in London to whom M. Casani attended personally', he
dismisses François or Josef or Mario with a nod, and settles
down to it with the great man himself. Probably they decide
to follow the sole with a *poulet en casserole* and an *omelette aux
fines herbes*; to the disappointment of the heroine, who lives
on a poultry farm in the country, and is going to tell her
younger sister all about it when she gets back.

No asparagus at dinner then. What about lunch? We flip
our way through a thousand novels, alert for the magic word,
and what do we get? 'Cold grouse and a salad, washed down
by a pint of Chablis.' Just that; always that. You and I, if I
may suppose you to have attended the same school of man-
ners, were taught not to drink with our mouth full, but, it
appears now, mistakenly taught. Perhaps, though, our teacher
never envisaged Chablis for us. It is with Chablis that an
obstinate mouthful is best washed down, and only when he
has so washed it down that the hero may 'carefully select a
cigarette'. You and I (to bring you in again) have little scope

for selection in our cigarette-case, provided that we left the bent one at home before coming out. But it may be—indeed, I think it must be—that the proofs of these novels get passed too hastily, and that what the author had intended was no more than this: 'Rochester drew out his dainty enamelled case and carefully selected a cigarette-end,' having had, we may suppose, a rewarding half-hour in the Park.

On this question, then, of asparagus (to come back to it with my collaborator's permission) we shall get no help from other so-called writers. We must do our own thinking. Now, if you live in the country, you can grow your own asparagus; or your gardener can grow his—however you put it to each other. At least you would think so. But it is not so easy. Theoretically an asparagus bed takes three years to mature. Practically what happens is that after the second lean year you decide, very naturally, to grow carrots instead (which also wave at the top), and after two years of carrots you decide, again very naturally, to give asparagus one more chance, and after giving it one more chance for another two barren years you decide on spinach, which doesn't wave, but gets down to it quickly. So in a little while you will have been trying to grow asparagus for eight years, and you will have come to the conclusion (as I have) that the thing cannot be done. You can buy asparagus, you can eat asparagus (Heavens, yes), but you can't grow it, and you can't read about it.

When I say that you can't read about it, I mean that you can't read about it unless I am writing. I shall continue, therefore, to write. There was a character in one of Anthony Hope's books who was of opinion that, though port tasted better without the conflicting aroma of tobacco, and though a cigar tasted better without the conflicting savour of port, yet port and a cigar together gave a better combined taste than either of them separately. Well, I feel the same way about asparagus and *Hollandaise* sauce. I am aware that such an announcement may get me into trouble with the *gourmet* and the *gourmand*. Resisting an attempt by my collaborator to digress into an examination of the exact difference between a *gourmet* and a *gourmand*, as to whether, for instance, it is or is not more marked than the difference between an egoist and an egotist, I shall tell these gentlemen that all which they are aching to say about melted butter is known to me. I remained unmoved. A man who loves *Hollandaise* sauce as I do must get at it somehow, and asparagus is the perfect vehicle.

As between French and English asparagus there is no argument. The French sort, which gives you a genteel suck at one end, and burns your fingers at the other, is not under discussion. Real asparagus must be eaten to the hilt, so that the last bite imperils the thumb. Now, however unemotional you remain during the encounter, however steeled your nerve, however steady your hand, yet tender fragments, precious seedlings, will crumble off from each shoot as you lave it in the sauce, and be left, green islets in a golden sea, marooned upon the plate. These must be secured at any cost—with the fingers, a spoon, a piece of bread, an old envelope, it matters not. When you are eating asparagus, you are eating asparagus. Reserve your breeding for the brussels sprouts.

As to the last inch of the stalk, whether you eat it or not, circumstances must guide you. It happens sometimes that, when husband and wife have helped themselves from a common dish and there is an odd number of shoots left, so that none can say whether the wife or the husband is to benefit, then they will fall to counting the thumb stalks upon their plates, whereby they hope to remedy any original unfairness

in the first helping. It will occur to you that, if you have dis-
posed completely of this or that number of stalks, then by so
much you will advantage yourself in any later re-adjustment.
For, in the presence of asparagus, a man must think for himself, and think quickly.

And now I would give you my 'Ode to Asparagus', but it
is not yet written, and time presses. Yet, since the earlier poets
have been (I suppose) too busy eating it to sing of it, I must
do what I can, if it be no more than four lines of tribute:

> Asparagus, in hours of ease
> A pleasing substitute for peas,
> When pain and anguish wring the brow
> The *only* vegetable, thou.

May brings not only asparagus but cricket. For what I was
worth (which was about 12, if the wicket was playing well)
I was a taught batsman rather than a natural one, and for any
success which failed to come my way I gladly give the credit
to others. I first came into contact with professionalism at
school, in what was known as the Colts' Net, being sent
there because, for my size, which was hardly observable, I
was a promising footballer, or, anyhow, ran about as if I
were. We were under the care of the chief professional—
Rudge, as I shall call him. Rudge had been bowling since the
days of Lumpy Stevens; they had obviously shared the same
sweater, now yellow with age and two sizes too short. When
one wondered what his county was, as, of course, one did,
one learnt that he had played for Durham, but only because

he had liked Durham, and in the face of spirited efforts by other counties to detach him. His length was perfect. He dropped the ball on the usual half-crown or postage-stamp, and mechanically told us to 'come out to it'. Without any difficulty we came out to it. Mechanically he then made the beginnings of a forward motion with a bent left elbow, which we glimpsed out of the corner of an eye as we replaced the stumps; a motion which seemed to say that, if we had come out to it like that, our stumps would still be intact. He continued to drop the ball on the same postage-stamp, we continued to play forward to it . . . and in a little while we were being spoken of as a candidate for our house eleven.

A year or two later I was introduced to a new professional. Rudge had retired, I suppose to Durham, and his place had been taken by (let us say) Whitworth. Whitworth was said to be in the Surrey Second Eleven, and only not playing for England because he preferred a coaching job. He bowled an extremely accurate fast-medium, also on a postage-stamp, but the stamp in this case was at his end of the pitch. It was quite impossible to 'come out to it' in the technical sense; so, having, as it were, nothing to go by, and feeling rather uncomfortable about the whole business, I hit his first ball to what would have been the Hotel if there had been no net, and if I had been batting at Lord's from the Nursery end. Nobody said anything, and we went on. He continued mechanically to pitch on his postage-stamp and I continued mechanically to find the Hotel. At the end of my quarter of an hour he said, very much impressed, 'Do you always hook good-length balls like that?' and I, thinking it unkind to disillusion him about his length, and unwise to say that I had only just thought of it, replied airily, 'Always.' He crept off in awe to speak to the Captain about it.

The Captain was the one man whom I could always bowl at the nets. He was, indeed, almost the only man I ever did bowl, most of my victims preferring to be caught spectacularly in the deep field after a succession of sixes. One day at the nets I bowled four straight balls in a quarter of an hour— I mean, I bowled the Captain four times in a quarter of an hour, and you can't do that without leaving an impression in the air that there is either a good bowler at one end or a bad batsman at the other. Naturally he preferred to think that there was a good bowler at my end; so that, with Whitworth solid behind me in the matter of hooking good-length balls, I was now to be regarded as an all-rounder and a candidate for the Eleven. As an all-rounder, I found myself in a very comfortable position. However unsuccessful I was (and I was) as a bat, there was always the hope that I would take a wicket one day, and however often I failed to do this (and I failed), there was at least the chance that some day I would make a run. An all-rounder suffers from none of those odious comparisons. Of course, Snooks is a better bat than Milne, but then Snooks can't bowl. Certainly Milne is not nearly such a good bowler as Crooks, but then Crooks doesn't profess to be a batsman. You see how easy it was.

As an all-rounder, then, I played for the School; and if the opposition had habitually consisted of six Captains, four Whitworths, and a wicket-keeper, I should have headed both the batting and bowling averages, and have been asked to play for Kent in the holidays. Unfortunately it never did, and, thus handicapped, I took the decision which was to affect my whole life. Should I be a professional cricketer, or should I just be a writer or something with a hook-stroke? I became a writer (or something) with a hook-stroke.

Now if you only have one stroke, it is obvious that, unless

Whitworths are always bowling, you have your 'off' days and your 'on' days; or to put it more clearly, lest you should think that I occasionally had some other objective than the Hotel, good days and bad days. During a spell of bad days eight of the fielding side would remain seated or chatting in groups when I came in, knowing that, if I did happen to get a contact, the catch would go to mid-on, and that if I didn't, the appeal for leg-before could safely be left to the wicket-keeper. But on my rare good days we had more movement. In one of those delightful Long Vacation matches at Cambridge, when justice at last is done, and an undergraduate can represent his college on his general charm of manner and prospects in the Tripos, there was a genuine Old Whit-worthian playing for the opposition. He had all the appur-tenances of a first-class Classic who was really a fast bowler; who would have struck Plato (if he had struck him) as really a fast bowler: a wicket-keeper standing twenty yards back, a thirty-yard run, half a dozen slips, and a Captain who didn't see how a fast bowler with all that could fail to get a wicket by tea-time. So we went on. My idea was to stay in until we had got all these slips in front of the Hotel, and it was a great pleasure to find that, even when they were all there, there was still room between two of them for a bicycle which somebody had left leaning against the rails. The rattle of the ball through the spokes of this bicycle marked the zenith of my career. Next over the bowler at the other end (why haven't we heard of him since?) sent down a half-volley dis-guised as a yorker. I stepped back to hook it, picked my feet with some difficulty out of the stumps, and returned to the pavilion.

Since then the supply of Old Whitworthians has run out, and I have had to do the best I can as a writer. Or something.

But I can still watch cricket; and watching cricket has given me more happiness than any other inactivity in which I have engaged. Lord's on a warm day, with a bottle, a mixed bag of sandwiches and a couple of spare pipes in a despatch-case, and I don't care who is playing whom. Cricket is the only game which I can enjoy completely without taking sides. Doubtless music-lovers get the same enjoyment from listening to a symphony without backing the first violin to beat the oboe, or both of them to outpace the conductor.

Nevertheless, I have been (I am told) lucky as a spectator of other games. I have only once seen the Wall Game at Eton, and then I saw a goal scored: a phenomenon which recurs, apparently, once every fifty years or so. And, at my only experience of an American football match, a player ran the whole length of the field to score a try (if that is what it was called); something which had not been done since Abraham Lincoln was a boy. This may surprise British rugby players, but normally the American game moves backwards and forwards by inches, stopping every now and then for the dead to be removed.

May brings not only asparagus and cricket, but the income-tax collector.

Between the wars, when the nations were (it was hoped) all being very united and peace-loving, it was suggested that the third verse of the National Anthem, which invited God to confound the politics and frustrate the knavish tricks of our enemies, was not a helpful contribution to European unity.

Alternative verses were offered by various people, the best of them, surprisingly, by Bernard Shaw. Meanwhile a writer to *The Times* had averted an immediate disruption by explaining that the notorious third verse dealt with domestic, not inter-national politics. The knavish tricks of the King's enemies were merely the knavish tricks and incitements to rebellion of the Stuart faction.

This being so, all danger of war now averted, I didn't see why the substitute verse shouldn't bring domestic politics up-to-date. So I submitted my own version.

> O Lord, our God, arise,
> Guard our securities,
>   Don't let them fall.
> Confound all party hacks
> Save those our Party backs,
> And make the income-tax
>   Optional.

This, though well-received privately, raised no public repercussions, and income-tax remained obligatory. I had done my best, but the economists were against me.

The payment of income-tax has produced for me the two perfect examples of muddled thinking. In 1920 I had had my first financial success with a play, and the local tax-collector was having his first financial success with me. This went on for some time; for, in those days, not only did one pay income-tax on an average of the previous three years, but, for some reason which I still don't understand, payment of the corresponding super-tax (as it was then called) was demanded a year later. Moreover, one had to make a separate return for this super-tax; so that in 1924, one was returning an income for 1920–21–22 which one had already returned a year earlier for income-tax. All this delving into the past was too much for me. When, as invariably happened, my returns differed, the Inspector would point this out in the kindest way, and add that, with my permission, he would accept my last year's income-tax return as the correct one for super-tax, even though, on two occasions, he lost by it. What then was the point of a second return in 1924 of one's 1920–21–22 income, if the Inspector knew about it already?

Utterly baffled, I made, as Calverley said, my 'woes the text of sermons in *The Times*'. This had two results. One was that a single return now serves for both income- and sur-tax: this being the only mark I have left (if, indeed, it was I who left it) on the British Constitution. The other was that an affronted Inland Revenue demanded an immediate re-statement of my income for the previous six years or so, just to show me where I got off if I criticized a Government department. I am glad to say that the accountant to whom, in despair, I now handed myself over, recovered about £300 which in my ignorance I had overpaid; thus showing Government departments where they got off if they tried to be too clever.

But the 'muddled thinking' was this. By 1924 pre-war prices and taxes had doubled; which meant, of course, that though everybody was asking for, and most were getting, higher pay, everybody was less well off. A gossip-writer, commenting on my letter in *The Times*, envied me the fabulous riches which allowed me to pay super-tax *'in these days!'* Super-tax in *those* days (before the war) had been paid on incomes above £5,000. Now it was paid on incomes above £2,000; and £2,000 took one about as far as £1,200 would have taken one in 1914. What was in his muddled mind? I suppose a vague feeling that anything super in such un-super days was indeed super.

The other example was this:

An agent wrote to suggest that I should contribute to a certain series of articles then appearing in an American magazine. The payment would be so-and-so. It was a staggering fee, which worked out at about six shillings a word. Now, as everybody knows, Americans write 'fifty dollars' as '50.00', putting the cents, whether there or not, after the decimal. It was probable that some of these noughts had lost themselves, and got in the wrong department; alternatively, that the dollars had been mistaken for pounds by the agent, and then multiplied by five to get them back to dollars. So I wrote back to ask for the correct figure, saying that nobody outside a lunatic asylum would be offering me six shillings a word. The reply was, in effect, this:

I have made further enquiries about the fee, and there is no doubt that I gave it you correctly. It is true that this works out at 6/– a word, *but you must remember that you will have to pay heavy income-tax on it in both countries.*

I never discovered the truth about that fee, because I decided that I didn't want to write the article anyhow. But I should like to make it clear to all other editors that I was *not* saying 'No, no, old man, you mustn't overpay me like this. I simply shouldn't know what to do with all that money.' They may put the decimal point as far to the right as they like, and they won't offend me.

I say this because authors notoriously get offended rather easily. When an actress is imitated on the stage, she is accustomed to watch from the front row of the stalls in the company of her press agent, laugh heartily and publicly, and then go behind to the impersonator's dressing-room and say 'Darling, you were wonderful!' I doubt if authors take parodies of themselves in quite that spirit. But there is a reason for this which parodist and public don't always realize. What the parodist looks for, and exaggerates, are the special words, phrases, tricks and mannerisms of the author he parodies. Thus in any parody of Wells one would use the word 'manifest' a good deal, bring in an 'athwart' or two, and make some play with dots . . . to give a few obvious (or manifest) examples. But every writer has, not only special words, phrases, tricks and mannerisms to which he has become devoted, so that now they come unsought to his pen, but also an equal array of words, phrases, tricks and mannerisms which he abhors, and which never have, and never will, come into his writing. Now, however well one knows a writer's books (and one must know them well in order to parody them well), one only knows what is inside them, not what is outside them. It is easy to discover that Wells was fond of 'manifest' and E. F. Benson of 'authentic'; but how would one know, if the one *never* wrote 'accordingly', and the other *never* began a sentence with 'and'? For this reason a parody which seems 'life-like' to the rest of the world may, by the inclusion of one wrong word, seem nonsense to the parodied. He is not amused.

I know nothing about painting, but I know what I don't like, and am not in the least afraid to say so. Many people who know nothing about writing are similarly fearless about my books.

The two stock criticisms of 'modern' painting and sculpture

are that, to the uninformed (like myself), they seem to have lost both form and meaning. The two stock answers are that Art cannot stand still, and that such recognized Old Masters, or Old Bores, as Binks and Jinks were once considered revolutionary, and look at them now. The two conclusions with which we are left are that to be unintelligible to the layman is to progress, and that progression is any movement, whether forwards, backwards or in circles.

When, in the company of an art critic, we contemplate a modern sculptor's latest masterpiece 'Niobe', and murmur foolishly that it isn't *our* idea of Niobe, and that surely no woman ever looked like that, however unhappy, we are told that this isn't one of Landseer's lions, which are so obviously lions, but the sculptor's abstract interpretation of Niobe, seen functionally, or in planes, or something; and we gather that this is a far, far better thing that he has done than Landseer ever did.

No doubt. But suppose one had begun at the other end? Suppose one had taken a block of stone, and hacked it about, and squared it off here, and rounded it there, and polished it, until it was a transportable size, ready for exhibition, but looking like nothing particular . . . and then said to one's wife, 'What shall I call it?' and one's wife, who was doing a crossword, said triumphantly 'Niobe!' And one called it 'Niobe'. You observe the difference; you observe how much easier it is if you go at it backwards. All the admiration you get for seeing in Niobe what no other artist has yet seen: for seeing her functionally, abstractedly, planispherically or whatever, and translating her thus into stone: all undeserved.

I write as a lifelong backwards artist. I draw a face: two eyes, a nose, a mouth and (if I remember them) ears. Then I look at it to see if it reminds me of anybody. If it is like old Snodgrass, and it must be like somebody, I write 'Thomas Snodgrass Esq.' underneath, and who is to know that I hadn't set out to draw him? If it is like nobody I know, then it must be exhibiting some emotion, and, after considering all the emotions, I label it 'Indignation'. Yet, somehow, at the back of my mind, I feel that it ought not to be as easy as this: that it used not to be as easy as this. 'The Last Supper' is obviously 'The Last Supper'; 'Mona Lisa' and the 'Laughing Cavalier' need no titles. Whistler's Mother could be his aunt, 'The Fighting Temeraire' any other ship of the line, and the picture would still give you all it had. But if the whole explanation of a work of art to the astonished layman is that the artist is interpreting something 'functionally', or by some inner light not granted to the layman, then the expert needs to know just what is being interpreted, if he is to appreciate it properly. In short, the title is now an intrinsic part of the work—as it used not to be.

I fancy that the test case for those of us who have read and delighted in *Green Mansions* is Rima. Once we understood the transmutation of Hudson's Rima into Epstein's Rima, then 'modern art' would be a new field of beauty open to us. But we should probably still ask ourselves silly questions. Suppose Hudson's Rima had in fact been described as a deformed and repulsive creature (and such creatures may well be met in a tropical forest), what shape would Epstein's Rima have taken; and, if the same, would it still have been a work of genius? And if it were now revealed that Landseer's commission for the base of Nelson's Column was 'Four Dolphins', and that what we have stupidly thought of as lions were not lions at all, but (obviously) abstract figures of dolphins, seen with the inner eye of the artist, would Landseer be respectable again? No, I suppose that that would be going too far. They should have been sea-lions.

All this is leading up to the sad story of my friend Tadema-Brown. The masterpiece which he was sending to the Spring Exhibition of his native town was entitled 'Diana Surprised While Bathing'; an old theme, generally represented by a good-looking female (Diana) surprised by an amorous male (Actaeon) when in the act of bathing. Tadema-Brown, being the artist he was, conceived it differently. He saw it as an atomic bomb (*disaster*) and an eyeball (*surprise*), in a surround of the earth's ecliptic (*love*—which makes the world go round). This, at least, was how I interpreted it when I saw the picture in his studio, and had got over my own surprise; but I understand that his friends, looking at it more broadly, acclaimed it merely as a bold severance from the classic tradition, and a dynamic exposure of the futility of modern civilisation. However this may be, the picture was sent to the Exhibition, but, owing to some mishap, it arrived without its title. The Secretary rang up Tadema-Brown, and hearing that he was in a nursing-home, decided to catalogue it himself. He took a good look at it, and called it 'Unknown Fish on Plate with Tennis Balls'; with the natural result that it was dismissed contemptuously by the critics as an outmoded piece of conventional still-life. So all the artist's genius went for nothing.

I feel that this should not be. However, I can do nothing about it. Let the Royal Academy now open, and be as modern as it pleases.

A T the end of the meadow into which our garden wanders
is a stream. This is called The River. Between the garden
and the meadow is a ditch. This is called The Brook. In front
of the house the brook has been widened between sandstone
walls into a piece of water forty yards long by four across,
and this piece of water is called The Stream. Now we know
where we are.

When we came here, the stream had no containing walls,
but followed an irregular course over the unlevelled ground,
so that here and there little islands showed themselves above
the water, and on these islands water-rats would polish up
their whiskers. It was all very rural, and sometimes I wish
that we had left it like that. But when the brook dried up in
summer, making the stream all island, one felt that somehow
a reserve of water must be kept in being. Could we collect
enough in a deepened, widened and walled-in stream to last
us through a drought? The question was never answered, for
it was at this moment that I discovered The Spring.

I forget who discovered the source of the Nile, but probably he felt much as I did when I scratched a way of escape
for the puddles on the sloping lawn which fell to the stream,

and found an hour later that the puddles were still full. This end of the little lawn had been a rubbish-heap when we came. We had cleared away the rubbish, and filled in the ground, but it had remained boggy and unpleasant. Now we knew why. So we dug out an irregular pool (The Spring) eight feet in diameter and four feet deep, lined it with sandstone, ringed it with limestone, dotted it with that stuff which looks like rhubarb but isn't, and gave it a channel into the stream; and, ever since, water has flowed down this channel at the rate of a thousand gallons a day.

To the simple-minded a thousand anything sounds a lot, and perhaps they are now picturing to themselves a foaming cascade leaping and tumbling on its way to the stream. Actually this does not happen. The overflow (as the arithmetical may discover) fills a glass in a little less than six seconds, which means that it is a pleasant, fair-sounding trickle. But the trickle goes on for ever. And though the brook does not conform to this literary tradition, feeling perhaps (and quite rightly) that what it would do for Tennyson, it certainly won't do for me, yet it does help to feed the stream all through the winter; sometimes, indeed, to repletion; and even in the summer it renews its activity after every rainstorm. In short, the stream may properly be described as running water; and at the east end, running out through a narrow opening in what must be called (still using these grandiloquent terms) The Stone Bridge, it becomes the brook again.

Into this stream we put a few goldfish. They made themselves at home in the weeds and reeds and mud, and we saw less of them than we had hoped. But they were not idle. Raking out the weeds one day, I found that I had brought up some little black-and-silver sparklets, which looked more like metallic fish than real ones. Gossip-writers tell us of well-known people who breed Corgis or Siamese cats; and though one suspects that it is the Corgis or the cats who do most of the work, one assumes that the so-called breeders are not taken by surprise. We were. I can think of no surprise more delightful than the discovery that a rake-full of weed taken from a rapidly congesting stream is alive with little silver fish. Of all Nature's bounties this seems for the moment the most bountiful. Suddenly the whole Universe becomes a possibility.

By the summer we had hundreds of goldfish in the stream, and on hot afternoons they lay about in glittering pools of light like a Turner sunset reflected in still water. We had other fish, not always identified, which came 'out of the everywhere' in that mysterious way only to be explained by Nature's abhorrence of a vacuum. Here was some not wholly occupied water, why not fill it? So she filled it with little fish and tritons and newts and water-beetles and everything else she could think of at the time, including grass-snakes.

One does not take kindly at first to grass-snakes. The big four-footers look horribly menacing in the water, as indeed, they are to the gentler inhabitants, and the babies, slow-worm size, are even more unlovable. I hoicked a big one out with a putter at our first acquaintance, and having knocked it on the head before it could collect itself and ask 'Where am I?' I went away to collect the family—my own family, I mean. When we came back, it lay there dead, with, by its side, a disgorged and elongated frog stretched out to nearly a foot in length. I felt sorry then for having killed it (and sorry, of course, for the frog), and have taken no action against grass-snakes since, save to hoick an occasional one out of the water—a sport little practised, but demanding a delicacy of approach, and an exact calculation of the centre of gravity of the quarry, unrivalled in other sports.

With all these fish in the water, the heron and the king-fisher have come and been welcome, earning their keep by the beauty they have brought. A pair of mallards have nested in the reeds; and once a swan found here a home from home. During a trial flight from a lake a few miles away it had developed engine trouble, and crash-landed in our little lane. We carried it down to the stream, and there it stayed for a few days, coming out occasionally to visit us through the open doors of the sitting-room. Having regained its nerve, and had a practice flight or two, it rejoined its family. But each year swallows play follow-my-leader down the length of the stream, touch and away; dragon-flies of every colour and size dart from point to point, and hover like helicopters; and from his home in the bank a water-rat launches himself silently, leaving no trace.

The strangest visitor to the stream was a stoat. I was in a deck-chair on the lawn, when it came from the rhododen-dron bushes on the opposite side of the stream, in search, it seemed, of a water-rat. Diving eagerly into the first hole it saw, it popped out, before it was quite ready, at the water end. Its enthusiasm slightly damped, it scrambled to land, shook itself, and went into the next hole. Once more a startled face shot into the stream; once more a dripping but still business-like back was climbing out. At the third hole, surely, somebody would be in. Nobody was. There was a third splash. And now, just opposite to me, it stood upright on its back legs, fingering its chin, and thinking back to the day when its mother had first told it about water-rats. Some-thing had slipped up. For a minute it stood there, wondering how it had got the thing wrong; perhaps it was rabbits, not water-rats; perhaps—and then, with a final shake, which seemed equally a bodily and mental dispersion of all this water, it dropped on to its fore-legs and stole back into the bushes.

So, one way and another, we have had great delight from our stream. But nothing lasts in a garden. There came a winter when the river rose to the top of its ten-foot banks and raced over the meadow; the stream merged into the general flood; and the rose-garden became a swimming-pool. Our goldfish left us and were last heard of at Sheerness. Then, on the day after the drive down from the lane had been re-surfaced with whatever chemical material was called for, the rains came, and poisoned water poured down the hill, and in the morning most of the natural inhabitants of the stream were dying or dead. Finally, the spring developed an oily orange scum, due to the iron in the water, and from being our pride was now our shame; so that we had to fill it in and cover it up, leaving only its outlet into the stream. But now the stream at that end became oilier, and scummier, and, because we had lost interest, more overgrown with weeds. Slowly the weeds and the scum moved towards the bridge, and even the water-rats deserted the banks, even the frogs came no longer to spawn. Well, we have had our fun from the stream. Nothing lasts in a garden, nothing stays the same. But something else takes its place. Perhaps one day it will be an orangery.

A great many words
Have been written about birds;
From rhapsody (Shelley's)
To more precise information about the colour of their bellies.

Unfortunately, bird books are either too descriptive or not descriptive enough. It is almost impossible to translate a bird's song into words, and easy, by insistence on colour, to give a false impression of its appearance. Chiaroscuro, rather than colour, identifies a bird for most of us; together with its size (particularly length of tail) and manner of flight. We can all recognize a swallow, once we have learnt its difference from a martin, but how many of us, seeing it in flight, would notice its red throat and green tail? A starling to the untutored eye is a black bird; not, as the coloured plate assures us, a spangled mixture of purple, green and blue. A detailed description of colour is only confusing.

As for the song, the bird books do their best, but the best is not very helpful. Just as it is easier to translate Latin into English than English into Latin, so it is easier to translate an identified song into words than to make the words identify the song. There should be some other notation than words, or than music for the unmusical. For instance: if a keen cricketer, verging on middle-age, were to ask me how to identify the song of the chaffinch, I should say 'Gover bowling'. Is there a cricketer in the house? Then he will know what I mean. The short quick steps to the crease and the final all-out effort as the arm comes over: this, and not the 'tissy-choo-éo' of the books is what the chaffinch is trying to imitate.

Civilization, as it is called, rings the changes from lustre to lustre, but one expects Nature to be more constant. Yet Nature, it seems to me, is not quite what it was when I was

young. The better sort of caterpillar, for instance, appears to
lead a less adventurous life. It stays quietly at home, instead
of roaming about as it used to, looking for company. Except
for the small green sort which one pinches in a rose-leaf or
removes from the hair beneath an oak-tree, and the larger
more crudely coloured sort which swarms on ragwort and
mullein, the caterpillar now plays no part in my life. In the
old days one was always being approached by something
good. Birds, too, are not what they were. Herons and king-
fishers, white owls and green woodpeckers bring exciting
moments; we even had a cormorant once, and I wrote to *The
Times* about it, as who would not; but something has happened to the simple companions of my youth. In the strip of
wood which bounded our old home blackbirds and thrushes
nested in every bush. Today, in spite of a superfluity of blackbirds and thrushes, and a housing estate for them many times
more spacious, fewer and fewer private dwellings are going
up. Are maternity homes now the fashion; or did the war-
time invasion of so many London children force them to
brush up their ideas on camouflage?

I hope that I am not giving anybody the impression that I
am trying to give him the impression that I am a true countryman, for it is only of late that I have lived wholly in the
country. I was born at the Kilburn end of Maida Vale, and
remained there until I was eleven. The family moved into
Kent, but by that time I was at school at Westminster. After
three years' exile at Cambridge, I returned to London in
order to be, or to try to be, a writer. A year in Whitefriars,
two years in Chelsea and seven years in Westminster convinced me that I should do better as a married writer, and
as such I lived until 1939 in my belovèd Chelsea. An American
woman, calling on us in this Chelsea house, did ask once if

we ever went into London, because, if so, would we dine
with her one evening at the Ritz; but she had come through
Knightsbridge in what is so mistakenly called the rush hour,
and had lost all sense of reality. Assuming with her permission
that Chelsea is London, I can claim to have been, with one
slight lapse and a war interval, faithful to my native town
for more than fifty years.

I was very fond of London; so fond of it, in fact, that I
liked it for what it was and not for what it might have been.
When I was a boy, or perhaps a little earlier, whiskered young
men called Edwin used to assure bashful young women called
Angelina that they were the most divine and peerless angels
in the world, without fault or blemish; and if Angelina suggested modestly from beneath drooping eyelashes that sometimes she feared that her temper was a little short (or her nose
a little long), Edwin would protest passionately that indeed
no, his darling was utterly, utterly perfect. This is one sort of
love. Cowper, less deeply enamoured, was inspired to say,
'England, with all thy faults I love thee still', which was very
handsome of him, though it was no way to talk to a lady.
However, no doubt he felt like that even about Mrs Unwin.
But the true lover neither maintains that the loved one is
faultless, nor feels the need to explain that he loves her in
spite of her faults. He recognizes the faults as themselves
objects of affection. With a more beautiful nose Angelina
would not be Angelina. It is her absurd nose which makes her
so much more lovable than Cleopatra. And that is just how
I have always felt about London.

The test question for the lover of London is to be found
on the Surrey side of the river. Before there was any talk of
Festivals, did you want to improve the Surrey side or didn't
you? If all those old wharves and warehouses were pulled

down—or, in the case of the wharve , pulled up—if all the
wharves and warehouses were destroyed, and a nice new
Embankment were built like the nice fairly new Embankment on the north side of the river, then we should have an
Embankment on each side of the Thames in London, just as
they have an Embankment on each side of the Seine in Paris.
Wouldn't that be nice?

For myself I cannot understand the passion for making
things, places, people like something or somebody else. The
only lasting virtue is individuality. The charm of London to
a lover of London is that it is not in the least like Paris; just as
the charm of Paris to a Parisian is that it is not in the least like
London. It is true that of this and that we may say that they
order these things better in France, but let us go to France
and watch them doing it . . . and then come back to London.
Don't ask me to tell you why I love the King's Road (there
is only one King's Road: down which Charles II travelled to
call upon his Nell in Chelsea); travel down it yourself from
Eaton Square to World's End, and tell yourself that of all
the unlovely roads . . . well, but think how many mothers
love unlovely sons, and wouldn't change them for the most
beautiful film star. Silly, but that is how we get to feel.

I am afraid that I have been carried away, as I always am
when I think of the vandals who would improve London into
something which was not London, and spoil my river for me.
For the London which I meant to write about was not a col-
lection of bricks and stone, nor a smudge on an atlas, but a
state of being. A man who confessed that he was living in Sin
might give the impression that he was some sort of an Anglo-
Indian, just as a woman living in Holy Wedlock could be
visualized as tucked away in Shropshire. It sounds much the
same whether you live in Luxor or Luxury, and a Yorkshire-

man could undoubtedly live in something like Idleness. Living in London has an equally deceptive sound at first hearing. 'So *that's* where he lives,' you say to yourself, when you should be saying 'So that's *how* he lives.'

The charm of London which remains, however often other people have written about it, is that one can live there as an individual and not as one of a community. I suppose that one is born with or without the communal feeling, and that to be born without it is to be uncivic, unpatriotic, selfish, and totally unworthy to be (as I rather think I am) Vice-President of the local Horticultural Society. Am I uncivic? Very well, then, I am uncivic. I can love a place without loving all the people in it; I can be proud of what its heroes have done without wanting to kiss them. (As they do in France, by the way.) For nothing can make me want to know people, just because they are handy. If I do meet them, I am as capable of liking them as anybody else, but I don't go about thinking, 'Oh, if only I could *meet* somebody!' as people with the communal sense seem to do. I prefer to choose my friends because I like them, not because they are neighbours; and if this means often enough that they don't choose me because they don't like me, well, how right they are.

In all the years when I lived in a flat I never knew the man below. It is true that I continually corresponded with him in (on my part) dignified and courtly phrases, beginning 'Dear Sir' and ending 'Yours faithfully', and explaining in between just why my bath-water came through his ceiling—a simple mathematical explanation, invoking the Law of Archimedes and the Law of Gravity, which I need not bother you with now. But I never spoke to him; and if I did meet him on the stairs or in the street, it was not to recognize him as the gentleman who was getting his head wet. In all the years

during which I lived in a London house I never knew my
neighbours on either side. On one occasion, in the household's absence, a burglar visited us and withdrew with a bag-
ful of loot. One of our neighbours, suspecting after ten years'
proximity that this was not the lawful owner coming out,
followed behind in some vague hope of giving evidence if a
policeman intervened, or of picking up the bag if it were
accidentally dropped. Whatever his intentions, he gave me
written information of the burglary (which, indeed, had
already proclaimed itself), and of the fact that he had so
nearly arrested the intruder. Naturally I wrote and thanked
him. But I still didn't know what he looked like.

Well, that was my London. I liked the look of it and the
feel of it and the blessed independence of it. I also liked much
of the entertainment which it offered. And since I would
rather read the news than have it read aloud to me, I liked
being able to go round the corner for a Late Night Final. I
didn't know the paper-man's name, nor he mine, but we
smiled at each other in a friendly way. I liked that too. I like
to be free to smile at the person who serves me, without
struggling to remember whether the baby is a boy or a girl,
whether lettuces or rheumatism should be the object of my
congratulation or concern. In short, I am damnably uncivic.

When Housman wrote

> Loveliest of trees the cherry now
> Is hung with bloom along the bough——

—did he mean that the cherry was the loveliest of all trees throughout the year, or only that it was the loveliest tree in the spring? Writing in prose, would he have said 'Loveliest of trees now, the cherry is hung with bloom', or 'Loveliest of trees, the cherry is now hung with bloom'? We have a large cherry tree standing between the house and the principal dahlia-bed. I place it thus because the First Gardener happened to comment to the Second Gardener one day on the beauty of the dahlias as seen from her bedroom window each morning, adding that of course she couldn't see it entirely because of the cherry tree. Later in the day she told me, with a little laugh at his devotion to dahlias, that he had suggested cutting out one of the bigger boughs so as to open up the bed for her in all its morning glory; a suggestion which I received with a much louder laugh. Unfortunately my laugh didn't get over properly, and in the winter, during my temporary absence in London, the bough was removed. The tree, which was indeed lovely during its brief blossoming, was now lovely but lopsided, and at the time of writing is merely lopsided. But even at its best it was never beautiful in summer or autumn.

(It has just occurred to me that I should like to read a novel called *Lovely But Lopsided*, though I doubt if it will ever be written.)

Balancing spring against autumn, remembering equally summer and winter, one cannot easily choose one's loveliest of trees. Blossom, I think, must be left out of the reckoning; but what of age? Is our chosen tree to be lovely all its life, or, like the oak, only when it is a veteran? If I limit myself to the trees which we have planted in our wood, I give the first place for all-the-year-round beauty to the silver birch; *Proxime accessit*, the larch; Honourable Mention, acacia and beech. No other tree can equal the spring green and autumn gold of the beech, but its summer dress is undistinguished, and throughout its youth it is gawky and without plan, like a girl at the awkward age. Our acacia, which comes into fairy-like leaf last of all, keeps its own exotic charm until the leaves fall, but thereafter becomes just a crude design for next year's exhibition. The silver birch and larch are shapely and beautifully alive, whatever the season.

The prize for ugliness is divided between the sycamore and the alder, trees which have been wished upon us. H. G. Wells once told the sycamore what he thought of it, and I shall not follow him. By a provision of Nature's which does not immediately advertise its advantages, the least desirable of her works are always the most prolific. One sycamore accidentally left in the neighbourhood will equip a householder with a sycamore grove in every bed; an alder by the river's brim a single alder was to him, but now is twenty more.

> Ugliest of trees, the ald and syc
> Are growing very much too thick:
> A house should be completely bald
> Of anything like syc and ald.

To return to our cherry tree.

It is one of life's little ironies that, unlike the British Empire, this is the only tree in the garden on which the blossom always sets. There are years when the apple trees are blossomless; years when apples and pears blossom, but nothing comes of it; and of course years when all Nature's endeavours bear fruit. But whatever the weather has been doing until June, in June our cherry tree is hung with cherries along the bough: along every bough: it is alight with cherries. When we first saw it so, we supposed foolishly that by the end of June we should be living on cherries; we saw ourselves (though personally I was against this) sending baskets of cherries away to our friends. But it was not so. Our cherry tree is too big to be netted, too prominent to be disfigured by other bird-resisting devices, and is now no more than the hired reception-room of the rooks' chattering cherry parties, '5–8 a.m., throughout June'. I used to believe that the ostrich and the booby were Nature's two silliest birds, but I know now that I was wrong. The rook is not only the most infuriating, but the silliest.

Let us consider first the ostrich.

This bird's reputation for silliness is based on its habit of burying its head in the sand, in the belief that it is thus rendered invisible to its pursuers. At first hearing this sounds somewhat foolish of it. There is, however, other evidence available than the legend of the nursery, which we should do well to consider. Ostrich-frequenters are unanimous in saying that in all their experience they have never seen an ostrich with its head buried in the sand. But isn't this exactly what the ostrich was counting on? It would be extremely silly of it to bury its head in the sand if its back view remained visible to all. But here we have the highest authorities agreeing that *they have never seen the back view of an ostrich with its head in the sand*; which is just the effect which the bird was trying to produce. Far from being silly the ostrich is now proved to have invented the most perfect form of camouflage. Other birds rely on Nature's provision for them; the ostrich worked it out for itself.

We pass on to the booby.

In the *Encyclopaedia Britannica* (to which any traces of erudition in this book may be ascribed) there is talk of 'a species of gannet known to sailors as boobies from the extraordinary stupidity they commonly display'. Rather surprisingly the matter is left there. Stupidity can take many forms, and one would have expected that, in fairness to the booby, the writer would have indicated where it fell short of the standard of intelligence expected of a sea-bird. For we must remember that what seems stupid to a sailor might not seem stupid to a gannet. Sailors cannot go about condemning a whole species of bird off-hand, just because it sees no difference between a rating and a ratline, and has never heard of Nelson. By the gannet's standard a sailor's inability to lay an egg or catch a fish in his mouth gives him very low marks for intelligence. Before we can judge, we must have more information.

Fortunately the *Twentieth Century Dictionary* supplies it. This describes the booby as 'a sea-bird of the gannet tribe, remarkable for its apparent stupidity in allowing itself to be knocked down with a stick'. Now no fair-minded investigator can regard this as conclusive evidence. If the bird were looking in the other direction, admiring the sunset, say, and thinking of its mother, and a sailor approached noiselessly from behind with a heavy stick, it would be a little unreasonable to say that the bird 'allowed' itself to be knocked down. Gravity rather than stupidity would be responsible for its ultimate position. But even if these birds are in the habit of looking sailors in the face, and are so appalled by what they see that they let themselves be knocked down when they could easily fly away, is this a proof of stupidity? The dictionary itself is doubtful. It speaks of the booby's 'apparent stupidity'. Mark that word 'apparent'. The booby, we are asked to believe, is not such a fool as it looks; there is design behind its apparent silliness. What the design is: whether this particular sort of gannet has lost its taste for fish (and, if so, who shall blame it?), and is now choosing the easiest form of suicide: whether it is working on a five-year-plan, leading sailors on until it has lured them into a complacent careless-ness which leaves them open to a counter-attack: what the reason is for their peculiar conduct we may never know. But if it comes to that, the whole tribe of gannets will never know why a sailor has 'Ever True dear Sal to You' tattooed on his chest. To a gannet it just seems silly.

Having, I hope, restored the reputation of the Ostrich and the Booby, I shall now consider Nature's silliest bird, the Rook.

My dictionary, which has been in a lamentable state of indecision all the morning, once again refuses to commit itself. It begins by defining the rook as 'a species of crow—from its croak', but realizing that it might just as well have described it as a species of horse from its hoarseness, throws in its hand and calls it impatiently 'a ruddy duck'; ending up, if you please, by defining it in human terms as 'a cheat; a sim-pleton', the one being the exact opposite of the other. Writ-ing a dictionary on these lines must be pretty easy work. But I do not need a dictionary to tell me anything about rooks. I know it all.

On the other side of the river there is a chicken-farm. With the details of the nauseous food laid out for the fowls in their pasturage I shall not sully my pen. It is enough to say that, loathsome as it is, it has an irresistible attraction for rooks. With, possibly, three or four elderly exceptions, all the rooks of Sussex now regard themselves as boarding across the river, with cherry-picking rights on our side of it. Living among rooks as I do, I have studied them carefully, hoping to find some clue to their mental processes. It is any day in the week. They are eating and squabbling among themselves as usual, when suddenly one of them comes sailing over the trees which line the river, and makes rapidly east.

1ST ROOK (*disengaging himself from the ginger-beer wire which had got entangled with his particular bit of garbage, and looking up*): Hallo! Where's Arbuthnot going?

2ND ROOK (*to the others*): I say, you fellows, where's Arbuthnot going?

3RD ROOK: He must be on to something!

1ST ROOK (CARMICHAEL): Get together, boys, Arbuthnot's on to something!

(*A cloud of them rises in the air and streams eastwards.*)

CARMICHAEL (*fussily assuming responsibility for the whole thing, as usual*): Now then, come along, come along! Sanderson, old man, just fly back and make sure that they all know. You take the north side Wilsborough, you whip up the stragglers on the south. Tell them that Arbuthnot's on to something.

Sanderson and Wilsborough wheel round and come back to us. A selection of cloth-heads turns and follows them, squawking 'I say, what's up? I thought we were going the other way?' Sanderson circles round to explain, forgets which way he was going and what he was going for, and makes for the north, accompanied by a few idiots screaming 'Where's Sanderson going?' Wilsborough shouts at them all, gives it up, and returns for fresh instructions from Carmichael.

Meanwhile Arbuthnot, three miles to the east, has managed to get rid of the soda-water stopper which had got mixed up with his swill, and, feeling more himself, returns for another helping. What is left of the pack hurries after him, picking up stragglers on the way, and telling each other happily that Arbuthnot is certainly on to something. In five minutes they are back at the chicken farm. Imagine their delight when they see all that food spread out beneath them! 'There!' they say triumphantly. 'Didn't I tell you? Food! One can always rely on Arbuthnot!' And they get down to it again.

Fools!

Twice in this book I have referred to the 'chatter' of rooks. The dictionary says that they 'croak'. We are both wrong. Their distinctive note is a querulous whine. I hear it outside my bedroom window from 5 to 8 every morning in June and early July. What have *they* got to whine about? I am the one who ought to complain. They are eating all my cherries.

Fools and Ingrates!

CONVERSATION, that idle conversation which starts nowhere and ends in the same place, requires two people,
one at each end. Listening is not enough.

Many years ago, and at this delightful time of the year
when the Season was in full swing in London, it would sometimes happen to a young man like myself that he would be
invited to a dinner-party. Now a dinner-party in those far-
off days was a solemn business. Dismiss at once from your
mind, young men of today, the picture of yourself, cigarette
between fingers, drinking gin-and-orange in the bed-sitting-
room with your host, while your hostess bustles in and out
of the kitchenette telling you that the soup is just coming in,
and have you ever tried veal loaf because it's rather fun—
'Oh, and Peter, could you do something constructive about
the pineapple chunks, because the thing you're supposed to
open it with doesn't seem to work.' It was nothing like that.

There would be nineteen people in the drawing-room
when the Shy Young Man was announced by the butler in
a loud authoritative voice as 'Mr Million'. The Hostess,
possibly remembering where she had seen him before, possibly not, would advance beneath a forest of chandelier and

over an acre of parquet flooring, to give him a languid hand
and say 'So glad you could come, let me see, I think you're
taking Miss Postlethwaite in, ah there she is, Muriel dear,
this is Mr Melon'—and there, poor devil, he was.

There were no cocktails in those days: nothing to loosen
the tongue, nothing to occupy the hands. Had Mr Melon lit
a cigarette, the ladies would have swooned and the men
muttered that it wasn't cricket; 'Parkinson', the Host, would
have said, 'remove Mr Mullins.' Smoking was for the dining-
room only, when the ladies had withdrawn. Mr Melon and
Miss Postlethwaite have to get on as best they can under
their own steam. This is what was known as the *mauvais
quart d'heure*. Once safely in the dining-room, they can eat;
now there is nothing they can do but talk. They are both
very shy, but, as Mr Melon knows only too well, the initiative is with the man.

MR MELON (*initiating*): Lovely day it's been, hasn't it?

MISS POSTLETHWAITE (*responding*): Yes.

MR M. (*following up*): Have you—er—have you been out
in it at all?

MISS P.: Oh, yes!

MR M.: One doesn't want to stop indoors on a day like
this.

MISS P.: Oh, no!

MR M. (*preparing the ground for his next remark: he had
worked this up in the hansom*): I always think that the flowers
in the Park are so pretty at this time of the year.

MISS P.: Yes, aren't they?

MR M. (*here it is*): Are you one of those people who know
all about flowers? (*This, he feels confidently, should be good for
five minutes.*)

MISS P.: No.

MR M.: Oh! (*Five seconds.*) I just wondered. (*Faint but pursuing, for it is not a subject which one abandons lightly.*) As a matter of fact I walked through the Park this morning on my way to the office.

MISS P.: Oh?

MR M. (*without much hope*): And also on my way back.

MISS P. Oh!

MR M.: The daffodils—— (*It occurs to him that there is not much to be done with daffodils, not at this time of the year, he was thinking of geraniums. Better initiate again.*) Er—have you seen any good plays lately?

MISS P.: No. (*Deciding, in a sudden spasm of self-confidence to develop this.*) Not lately.

MR M.: Oh! (*He is not sure how to take it. Has she been in bed with a cold, or is dramatic art letting her down just now?*) I saw 'The Balcony Girl' the other day.

MISS P.: Oh?

MR M. (*doing his best for dramatic art*): Very good, I thought. (*Apologetically:*) If you like that sort of thing.

MISS P.: Yes, I suppose so.

MR M. (*realizing from this that she is a highbrow, and adapting himself like lightning to the changed atmosphere*): Did you read that article in the *Fortnightly* last month by William Archer?

MISS P.: No, I don't think so.

MR M.: Oh, I just wondered.

MISS P.: No, I'm almost sure I didn't.

MR M.: It was about—er—Ibsen, discussing his influence on the modern stage and—er—all that.

MISS P.: Oh, yes? (*She assumes the earnest expression of one who can't wait to hear what Ibsen's influence on the modern stage and all that has been, but it is overlaid by the expression of one who rather thinks that her off fore suspender is going; and the moment passes.*)

MR M. (*despairingly*): I just wondered. Er—have you——

MISS P. (*simultaneously*): Have you——

MR M. I beg your pardon!

MISS P. (*simultaneously*): I beg your pardon!

MR M. (*getting in first this time*): Please go on.

MISS P. It was nothing. What were *you* going to say?

MR M. Oh, nothing. I just wondered——

THE BUTLER (*loudly*): Dinner is served!

MR M. (*to himself, but less quietly than is usual in good society*): Thank God! (*He offers her his arm, and they take their place in the queue which troops down the big staircase to the dining-room.*)

Now it is easy to see what is wrong with this conversation. The man's end is working well, but the woman's end has no bounce. A pudding of a girl, Miss Postlethwaite, I fear, and if her stockings come down, no one need feel sorry for her. Still, she was young then; she was very shy; it was her first dinner-party. Let us consider how Miss Hepplewhite, now in her third season, would have made out.

MR MELON: Lovely day it's been, hasn't it?

MISS HEPPLEWHITE (*ecstatically*): Lovely! I always say that there's *nothing* like the summer. It's so—so *different*! Have you been enjoying it, or did you have to sit in a stuffy old office all day?

MR M.: Well, I——

MISS H.: I always feel so sorry for men, having to work in an office on a day like this, when all Nature is calling to them to come out. Particularly in the summer-time, I mean there's something *about* the summer, isn't there, which gets into one's blood and sets every nerve tingling. *Did* you

happen to notice the geraniums in the Park, or don't you
go that way at all?

MR M.: Well, as a matter of fact——

MISS H.: I make a point of walking round the Park every
morning during the Season. I don't feel that the day has
really begun until one has been once round the Park. Don't
you agree with me?

MR M.: Well, as I was saying——

MISS H.: Now what were we talking about? Oh, of
course, the geraniums. You may think it funny of me, but
I must say I *prefer* daffodils. I *adore* daffodils. I always think
when I see them of those wonderful lines of Wordsworth's:
'My heart leaps up when I behold the dancing daffodils.' So
true, isn't it?

MR M.: I think the actual lines——

MISS M. (*deciding to drop Wordsworth*): Have you been to
any interesting plays lately?

MR M.: Well, I——

MISS H.: There's something about a play which makes it
so utterly *different* from a novel. I mean it's another experience altogether. I saw one the other night—now what was it
called . . .

Well, who cares, and she'd probably get the name wrong
anyway. Miss Hepplewhite, you observe, is by no means a
pudding. Keeping our metaphor in the kitchen, we might
perhaps describe her as an escape of gas. Poor Mr Melon is
doing his best to turn the tap off, but each time he gets near
he is blown away again. The result is hardly idle, for Miss
Hepplewhite is obviously working under full pressure, and
it certainly cannot be called conversation.

But Mr Melon, much as I regret to say it, was also at fault.
You remember that when Miss Hepplewhite confused the

rainbow, at which Wordsworth's heart leapt up, with the
daffodils, at which it merely filled with pleasure (and there
is a world of difference, as you can try for yourselves, between being full and leaping), Mr Melon started in to correct
her. Now that was all wrong. The standards of idle conversation are not the standards of the classroom. Accuracy is
not called for. Each partner must adapt himself, or herself,
to the other, assenting with an agreeable nod to any statement however misfounded. An experience of my own will
explain what I mean.

The other day I found myself talking with a stranger in a
restaurant-car; or, more accurately, I found him talking to
me. With little effort on my part the conversation had moved
from some such obvious starting-point as the ineluctability
of egg sauce in the after-life of the cod to the case of a friend
of his who had thrown up an erratic income, which occasionally reached £5,000, for an assured one of £1,500 with a
pension to follow. At my suggestion that his friend had made
the wrong choice, he said, 'Oh, come now, in these days
how many of you fellows in the City can count on a regular
£1,500 a year?' Naturally I agreed with him that very few
of us fellows could, the City being what it was just now;
and before we reached Paddington he had a clear view of
me as a junior partner in the flourishing firm of Peabody,
Peabody & Stickle. Taking our metaphor this time from the
stable, we may say that idle conversation should be ridden on
the snaffle and not on the curb; it should be allowed its head.

So, dear lady, if your companion of the moment, under
some misheard direction of your hostess, talks to you as if
you had been in the Wrens during the war, don't contradict
him. Just be as nautical as you can without overdoing it. To
say, 'Well, *actually* I don't know much about coaling at sea,

because I was in the Land Army' brings the conversation to
a sudden stop. Your companion has to readjust his ideas,
forget all the amusing things he was going to say about
bollards, and pump up something about the beet subsidy.
This is hard work, not idleness. Of course there is no need
to pursue the one subject all the time, nor any reason why
you should not initiate a little for yourself. For instance: at
a moment when talk about stays was taking you a little out
of your depth, and making you wonder what you would be
into next, it would be quite in order for you to say: 'Yes,
don't they? I was always so thankful that I didn't go into the
Land Army. A friend of mine was telling me——' and there
you are, safely back in the byre. In a little while you will be
able to mention that in fact you did have a couple of years
yourself with Farmer Whackstraw before taking to the boats.

Possibly some of you may think that the brilliant chatter
which you have heard on the stage in such plays as—well,
we needn't mention names—is the perfection of idle conversation. Believe me it wasn't idle. Blood, sweat and tears
went to the making of it. The perfect idle conversation takes
place without preparation, without effort, between two
people of equal minds and equal idleness. Given these conditions there is no difficulty about it. In a last attempt to be
helpful, let me record the complete example:

(*The Husband is in an armchair with 'The Times'. The wife is
on the sofa, reading 'Gone With the Wind' for the tenth time.*)
HUSBAND (*breaking a half-hour silence*): What's a flower in
seven letters beginning with—oh, it's all right, I've got it,
Nigella.
WIFE (*roused from her book and looking up*): Put a log on
the fire, darling. What did you say?

HUSBAND: Nothing. Sorry. Didn't notice you were reading.

(*He throws a log on the fire, and returns to his crossword. A happy silence descends on them again. Scene closes*)

In 1918 my first full-length play, *Belinda*, had a short run at the New Theatre. In the summer of 1923 Laurence Langner, of the New York Theatre Guild, came to England to talk to Bernard Shaw about the American production of *Saint Joan*. As the Theatre Guild had produced one or two later plays of mine, he looked in on us at our Chelsea house to say how-do-you-do; and he suggested, when he left, that I should accompany him to the Adelphi, and so meet Shaw for the first time. Doubtless he had some good reason for asking me to come with him, doubtless I had some good reason for agreeing to go; but I am in a state of complete bewilderment now as to what those reasons could have been. If ever two people were a business company, and a third was an anti-climax, this was the occasion. However, I went.

I don't know whether this was also Langner's first meeting with Shaw, but at least he was expected, welcomed, and in a position to introduce me.

Shaw held out his hand, and said eagerly, as if he had been brooding about it for five years, and was glad to get it off his mind: 'You know, your Belinda was a minx, that's what she was, she was a minx!'

Naturally I was surprised that he had seen a play of mine, sorry that it had not been a later and a better one, flattered

that he remembered it and identified me as the author, and
not at all hurt by his estimate of its heroine. In acknowledge-
ment I said something less than all this (as it might have been
'Oh?'), and Shaw and Langner then got down to business.
I may have been given some photographs of Grecian ruins
to look at in a quiet corner, or I may have said 'Well—I—
er——', and left. I cannot remember.

About three years later I met Shaw again. This time I was
the least important guest at a Men Only dinner-party, given
in his honour by Sir Henry Norman. On my arrival I was
presented to him; and he said eagerly, as if he had been
brooding about it now for eight years, and was determined
to get it off his mind:

'You know, your Belinda was a minx, that's what she was,
she was a minx!'

There was no need nor time to say anything, for others
were waiting to shake hands with him. At dinner I sat at
the opposite end of the table. After dinner we were joined
by various women all eager to meet him, and he was
swallowed up. We had no more conversation, then or
ever.

I said that I was not hurt at the accusation that Belinda
was a minx. I am not sure that 'minx' is the exact word for
her, but if it conveys the sense of an incorrigible, middle-
aged 'flirt' (as she would have been named in those days)
with all the charm of Irene Vanbrugh: or the 'maddening
woman' which her husband called her lovingly: then it will
do. In any case it doesn't matter what you call her. She was
the heroine of a purely artificial comedy whose only purpose was to amuse, and she herself no closer to reality than
any character in, say, *The Importance of Being Earnest*. In
short, she didn't exist. A minx, was she? Well, what I wanted

to say to Shaw at that second meeting was 'And how about Candida?' For that did matter. Candida does exist.

All through the play Morell (the husband) and March-banks (the lunatic, the lover and the poet) are exchanging unpleasant truths about each other, and Candida is telling them both unpleasant truths about themselves. But nobody, not even the author, tells the unpleasant truth about Candida, nor seems aware of it. So, one night, having then seen and read the play half a dozen times, and being unable to put up with Candida's complacency any longer, I pushed my way into the sitting-room of St. Dominic's Parsonage just after the curtain had fallen. Candida, you remember, has been asked to choose finally between husband and lover, and has dramatically chose 'the weaker of the two'. Morell, like most of the audience, thinks that this means Marchbanks, and accepts his defeat and loss of Candida 'with the calm of collapse'. But it is the lover who has lost. And so, when I come in, husband and wife are alone, and in each other's arms. 'But', says the author, 'they do not know the secret in the poet's heart.'

CANDIDA (*releasing herself calmly as I come in*): Yes?

ME: I wonder if you could spare me five minutes?

CANDIDA: James dear (*he is still a little bewildered by the surprising end of the play*)—here's a gentleman come to see you. From the Tower Hamlets Freedom Group?

ME: Er—no. Not exactly.

CANDIDA: Ah, then the Mile End branch of the Social Democratic Federation. James dear! The Mile End branch.

MORELL: Yes, Mr—er—you wish to see me?

ME: It was you, Mrs Morell, that I wanted to speak to.

CANDIDA: Me? But I know so little about these things. I leave all that to my husband's secretary. (*Understanding suddenly, and brightening.*) Or did you wish to see me privately?

MORELL: You are an old friend of my wife's, sir?

ME: I met her first about ten years ago. If I might be allowed——

CANDIDA (*with her usual competence*): James, dear, your lecture on Thursday to the Land Restoration League—just five minutes' final polishing in the dining-room?

MORELL: Yes, I think perhaps—then, if you will excuse me, Mr—er—— (*He goes out.*)

CANDIDA: There! Do sit down, won't you? Let's be comfortable anyhow. (*Cosily, as she sits down.*) Now tell me all about it!

ME: Thank you. (*I sit down.*) Mrs Morell, I couldn't help overhearing what took place just now between you and your husband and Marchbanks.

CANDIDA: Poor little Eugene! I hated sending him away. Fancy your overhearing!

ME: I really couldn't help it; you all spoke so loudly, almost as if you wanted everybody to hear. You know, I thought you did it very well.

CANDIDA (*surprised*): Did what?

ME: Made your choice between them. (*Dramatically:*) 'I give myself to the weaker of the two.' Very impressive.

CANDIDA (*not quite sure how to take this*): Oh! Don't you think I was right?

ME (*with conviction*): To choose James? Undoubtedly.

CANDIDA (*complacent again*): He *is* the weaker, you know. All he said about his 'strength for my defence', his 'industry for my livelihood'—well, it sounded very fine, everything James says *does*—but he would be quite lost without me. He depends on me entirely. Now Eugene——

ME (*quoting him*): 'My weakness, my desolation, my heart's need!'

CANDIDA (*explaining proudly, in case it had been over-looked*): Poetry, you know. He's always so poetical. But he doesn't really *need* me as my husband does.

ME: Haven't you got it wrong, Mrs Morell? Don't you mean that you don't need *him* as you need your husband?

CANDIDA (*hurt*): I don't think you understand.

ME: Every Candida can find as many Eugenes as she wants, and every Eugene as many Candidas. But honest, industrious, faithful husbands aren't to be picked up so easily.

CANDIDA: Picked up? (*With a wrinkle of distaste:*) What a horrid way of putting it!

ME: And a silly one—I'm sorry. I meant to have said 'captured'. Pursued, run down and captured.

CANDIDA (*indignantly*): Are you suggesting that I *ran after* James?

ME: I am.

CANDIDA: I've never heard anything so ridiculous! James was frantically in love with me.

ME: In the end, yes. But at first—— Don't you know your Shaw?

CANDIDA (*shaking her head*): Ought I? Shaw . . . Shaw. Oh, is he that rather wild-looking Socialist who sits on my husband's platform sometimes?

ME: Bernard Shaw, our greatest living dramatist. You must have read or seen his plays.

CANDIDA (*with a disarming smile*): I'm so busy with the house and the children and James—he's just like one of them, you know—and then, of course, Eugene, but I *will* read him if you think I ought to. Where can I get his book?

ME: Never mind now. But you could try a bookseller some time.

CANDIDA: Does Mr Shaw say I ran after James?

ME: Shaw says that it is every woman's business to get married; that in her search for the security of marriage she always takes the initiative; and that, contrary to the general belief, Woman is the pursuer and Man the pursued.

CANDIDA (*after a long pause*): Well . . . (*with a secret smile*) I do see what he means.

ME: If you don't mind my saying so, Mrs Morell, you came from a very unattractive home. Your father——

CANDIDA: Poor Papa!

ME: Poor, but dishonest. Uneducated, unmannered, uncultured. That was your humble background. And there was this handsome, eloquent young clergyman from a different social class, all the women in love with him, women in his own circle far above yours, all eager to marry him. And you Candida Burgess, old Burgess' daughter, beat them all at their own game, and carried him off—don't tell me you take no credit for that.

CANDIDA (*smiling reminiscently*): Well, I——

ME: Pursued, ran down and captured.

CANDIDA (*archly*): Captured his attention, shall we say?

ME: Very well, leave it at that. And now, here he is at forty, all set to be a Bishop.

CANDIDA (*eagerly*): Do you really think so? (*Anxiously:*) You don't *know* anything?

ME: I know that he is the type from whose fount all Bishops spring. There is no man in London more certain to be a Bishop.

CANDIDA: Well, I do think he would make a very good one.

ME: And you a very good Bishop's wife.

CANDIDA (*primly*): I hope I shall do my duty.

ME: I am sure you will. And now, Mrs Morell, I beg you for once to be as candid as your name. A little while ago you were asked to choose between two suitors. On the one hand a man of forty, your lawful husband, who was already giving you a station in life far above that into which you were born, and a security which from your childhood you had never had; a man solidly established, with the highest prizes of his calling within reach; the father of your children. On the other hand, an unstable boy of eighteen, earning nothing, and dependent for a bare living on a family which would never tolerate the ridiculous marriage he was offering you: a marriage for which the husband could provide no better support than the charity of a father-in-law who might at any moment be in gaol. Yet in making the obvious choice, the only choice for a sensible woman, you had the nerve to pretend that you were giving yourself (how nobly!) to the weaker of the two! . . . You meant the richer of the two, didn't you? (*Candida is silent.*) Come on! I won't give you away to your husband.

CANDIDA (*indignantly*): How dare—— (*She stops suddenly, and says with a maternal smile:*) Poor James! Men *are* such children, aren't they?

ME: And have to be humoured?

CANDIDA: Day by day, hour by hour, minute by minute!

ME: So you have humoured James by leaving him more than ever convinced of the nobility of his wife?

CANDIDA (*simply*): Of course! It was my duty.

ME (*finding this unanswerable, and getting up*): All my congratulations. But you didn't fool them both, you know.

CANDIDA: What *do* you mean?

ME: James, yes. Not Eugene. *That* was 'the secret in the poet's heart', the secret which he hid from you and your husband.

CANDIDA (*proudly*): Eugene had no secrets from *me*.

ME: Only this one. Because he only discovered it at that last moment.

CANDIDA: And what did he discover, Mr Knowall?

ME: That his Candida was just an ordinary self-deceiving, self-centred, self-protecting, complacent, attitudinizing— there's a short word for all that, if I could only think of it. Not quite 'minx', but——

CANDIDA (*rising with dignity*): I think you had better go now. You have said quite enough.

Yes, perhaps I have. But I shall just add that my admiration of Shaw is such that I would gladly give twenty *Candidas* for one *You Never Can Tell*.

When I was about the size of a lupin, I had my first intro- duction to British garden flowers. This took place in Vic- torian London, where I scraped an acquaintance, so to speak, with the inevitable geranium, lobelia and calceolaria. They sat in small round beds behind an edging of up-ended blue-black tiles like the edging of a blanc-mange, the lobe- lias drooping to the gravel, the geraniums, hot and red, in the middle, the calceolaria roaming over the spaces in between.

On one day we had a tilting-ground for cats; on the next

we had a circle of flowers; it was as simple as that. I now knew the answer to that question which London children so often asked their mothers: 'Mummy, where do flowers come from?' Nurserymen brought them in their little grey wheelbarrows. However, when I was twelve we moved into the country, and it was not long before I realized how absurdly innocent I had been. Abandoning the wheelbarrow theory, I applied my knowledge of the facts of life, and deduced, more or less accurately, what went on in a garden. I accepted it without embarrassment.

Moreover, like most schoolboys, I accepted it, and the garden, without interest. In the Easter holidays there was not much there, and in the summer holidays there was so much else to do. Owing to this absurd craze of the elderly for Education, one missed three of the four big months in a garden's life: May, June and July. Even in August flower-beds figured most potently as forbidden ground for cricket-balls, tennis-balls and croquet-balls, and deterrents, there-fore, of a fine, free style. One's heart was in the kitchen-garden.

It is the recurrent problem of the garden-owner to decide which of these four months shows his garden at its best. Each month we exchange old beauties for new ones, but never can be sure whether we have gained or lost on the exchange. Rose garden for rock garden, dahlias for delphin-iums, lupins for tulips, azaleas for daffodils, if we could have them all together, what a wealth of loveliness it would be. Since we cannot, which month shall we choose, if, much too grandly, we 'throw the gardens open' to the public, or, more modestly, just throw a small party? Each year the problem recurs.

Once I made a list of my ten favourite garden flowers in

order of preference. Here it is, slightly revised, and dated by its best month:

1. Daffodil.   (April.)
2. Polyanthus.   (April–May.)
3. Delphinium.   (July.)
4. Tulip.   (May.)
5. Lupin.   (June.)
6. Dahlia.   (August.)
7. Zinnia.   (August.)
8. Phlox.   (August.)
9. Rose.   (June–July.)
10. Sweet William.   (July.)

It occurs to me now that I ought to write them in the reverse order; and that what matters more than the order is that I have left out the two best, Aubrietia and Lithospermum, perhaps because walls and rock gardens want a list of their own; as, of course, do flowers for the house, with gladioli and sweet peas at the head. I have left out lilac and azaleas. Also marigolds should come in, if only for the name and their indefeasible habit; and wallflowers and snapdragons would if we were more lucky with them. No, it is impossible to set one against the other, when they are all lovely, and when there is more difference between varieties than between species; impossible to decide on any one of the four months as the best. What I am really looking for is a weedless month.

I shall now make a list of my ten most hated weeds:

1. Bindweed.
2. Ground Elder.
3. Dandelion.

4. Ground Elder.
5. Bindweed.
6. Bindweed.
7. Ground Elder.
8. Bindweed.
9. A curious kind of reed which climbs from the stream into the rock garden and can't be pulled up because it is built in sections like a Bailey bridge and each section comes away in your hand.
10. Bindweed.

After years of struggle I have decided that the only thing you can do with bindweed is to pretend to like it. Unfortunately I don't like white flowers anyway.

One of the advantages of being disorderly is that one is constantly making exciting discoveries. In one room or another I have a dozen drawers full of manuscripts, typescripts, trade-agreements, press-cuttings, old letters, old cheques and pass-books; which have collected themselves over the years, and have been rioting together ever since. It is impossible to look for anything, without finding something else of more interest, if not at the moment of more urgency. This morning I was searching for a copy of a play, and found myself reading a letter: a letter addressed not to myself, in a handwriting unknown to me. It surprised me a good deal. However, as there was nothing private in it, I can do no harm by reproducing it here.

Nov. 20th, 1886

MY DEAR MAMA,

　　We went to Hamstid Heft yestoday. We
had a sanambil. We had piggy-backs.

　　I want sme tools ples Mama
lost of x x x x

　　　　　You loving

　　　　　　　ALAN

This must have been the first letter which I ever wrote,
for only so would it have been preserved so carefully. It was
written at the age of four from my kindergarten school. I
never did like collaboration, and it is clear that I spurned it
on this occasion. All around me (I like to think) were other
little boys and girls writing to their dear mammas; asking
their companions how to spell Hampstead Heath, or waiting
glassy-eyed for some suggestion from the mistress as to what
constituted 'a letter'. I just sailed ahead, tongue out, arms
outspread. We had had a sanambil, and I had decided to be
a carpenter. The family would expect to be told.

If anybody else has ever had a sanambil, I should like him
to get in touch with me. The word is clearly written, the
'bil' heavily inked over; as if I had played with the idea of
some other ending, but realized in time that this combination
of letters was the most informative. Could I have meant a
'scramble'? One from whose pen 'piggy-backs' flowed so
faultlessly would surely have made a better beginning of it.
Well, we shall never know now; but I like to think of it as
one of those pleasant Victorian games, now gone with so
much else of those days which was good.

OF all the Bank Holidays the First Monday in August seems the most genuine. Boxing Day is too closely attached to Christmas, as Easter Monday to Good Friday, for the individual bounty of either to impress itself on the mind. Whit Monday, like Easter Monday, moves with the times under some mysterious compulsion of the moon. One cannot look forward to it until one has remembered when it is going to be. But the First Monday in August depends upon nothing but itself. It is a gift-day, out of, and generally under, the blue.

Bank Holidays were invented by Sir John Lubbock. He also invented the Bee (with a little help from Maeterlinck) and the Hundred Best Books. A full life. There are four Bank Holidays in the year, which may be described loosely as holidays for banks. To a foreigner the first sight of all these people from banks lying on the beach, and forming what is known as a sterling area, must be very impressive; and it is only when he has stood in a *queue* for an hour, waiting for a sail in the *Skylark*, that he realizes that some of the smaller ones are not bankers. 'What then,' he asks himself, 'is the definition of a Bank Holiday? What distinguishes it from any other kind of holiday?'

The answer is simple:

No person is compelled to make any payment or do any act upon a Bank Holiday which he would not be compelled to do or make on Christmas Day or Good Friday, and the making of a payment or the doing of an act on the following day is equivalent to doing it on the holiday.

A Gallup Poll inquirer at Victoria Station, who asked a number of hot people just arriving from Margate if they realized that it was to this that they owed their enjoyment of the day and the fact that their noses were beginning to peel, recorded the following distribution of opinion:

'Wossat?'	92%
'Ur.'	7%
'Sorry, I'm a stranger.'	1%

Since your own answer is not likely to be any more rewarding, we will pass on.

Why should men in banks have these special holidays? Or is the answer that they don't? There are many things about banks of which I am ignorant, and this, I now see, is one of them. Let us consider it. Bank clerks, presumably, have the annual holiday of other workers: 'staggered', so that there may always be somebody there to cash our modest cheque for us or inform us reproachfully that we are overdrawn. Are 'bank holidays', then, just days when the doors are closed to the public, while the bank is a private hive of industry, finding out how much money it has? Otherwise I don't see how it could ever find out. When, with a great deal of indiarubber, the Sub-manager has just made it £1,847,632 10s. 5d. for the second time, how annoying for him if we were to choose that very moment to pay in £5 17s. 6d. and to draw out £1 2s. 9d. More indiarubber.

More finger exercises. One's work would never be done. So it was decided (this is what we think now) that banks should have these four undisturbed days in the year in which to settle their own acccunts, and that these days should be called 'holidays'; so that, while other people were enjoying them, the banking world could at least have a good, hollow laugh.

And this leads us to the question, Do other people enjoy them? Of course, any man enjoys a day's holiday; and when he came home to his wife last Saturday, it was delightful to know that he wouldn't have to go back to the office until Tuesday. But would (or wouldn't) any other Monday have been a better day? How many people prefer a crowded beach, park, zoo and train to an uncrowded one? How many people like congestion for its own sake? Numbers are re-assuring, certainly, but there will always be somebody else. Is a man less lonely in his soul if there are thousands of others all perspiring like himself in pursuit of the same pleasure?

Perhaps another Gallup Poll would tell us the answer. I can't begin to do it, because, hating crowds as I do, I have no right to speak for them. Moreover, I have been lucky enough, for the most of my life, to have been my own dictator; and even in those earlier years when I attended an office, it was the office of a weekly paper which made a holiday of every Monday. So a Bank Holiday has always been to me just a day when roads were unpleasantly crowded, shops were shut, and letters and papers might or might not come; a day of which one was glad to see the end.

Selfish? No. Just a personal feeling such as may still be expressed in this country; but a feeling shared, I imagine, by thousands of park and zoo keepers, waiters, railway porters, bus conductors and policemen, for whom a Bank Holiday is no holiday. Whatever delight is to be found in a crowd, they find it not. In these days, when the Government's guiding principle seems to be 'If everybody can't have it, then nobody shall,' an institution which creates so many unprivileged is asking for notice. As soon as the axe falls, I shall put forward my plan for a real Bank Holiday. A holiday which you can bank.

We pay money into a bank so that we may take it out as we need it. Let every man, woman and child have the right to pay four special days into the holiday bank, to be taken out when most wanted. The average worker has his holiday suited to the convenience of his employer; over these four days the employer would hold no lien. In most Government offices this system is already in effect for the annual holiday, which may be taken in single days or in one period as and when the employee pleases. No doubt this is why Government offices have to have such a large reserve of crossword-solvers and tea-drinkers. But four free days of one's own choosing, taken in single days, would not inconvenience the most understaffed office. And these days would be real banked holidays. . . .

Bees and the Hundred Best Books are always with us, but it is not until this month that wasps call attention to themselves. One of the astonishing things about wasps is that the Queen is responsible for 80,000 other wasps; and the next most astonishing thing is that when I kill a queen in May, nobody notices in August that there are 80,000 wasps less. In one May a little while ago I killed fifty queens, diminishing the wasp-in-marmalade ration by four million. One did feel vaguely in the following August that there were fewer wasps about, but one would have expected a deficit of four million to have made more of a mark on one's consciousness.

My particular hunting-ground for queen wasps is among the rhododendrons. I kill them as they come out backwards from the calyx of a flower, snapping them between a matchbox and a spectacle-case. This requires very accurate timing, as one must take them in mid-air in order not to crush the blooms. As I say, I killed fifty in one season, not counting those damaged and unlikely to reach their base, or, if reaching it, unlikely to take any further interest in motherhood. It sounds dangerous work, but I have only been stung once —by an unsuspected nettle which had strayed into the bed.

How heedless one has always been over the tragedies of insect life. One never wearies of killing wasps and ants and flies—mothers on a much larger scale than the thrush, whose deserted nest fills us with remorse that we pried into it. In youth, relying on some naturalist who had had no personal experience to guide him, we told ourselves that 'insects don't feel pain'. For some reason this comforted us in our pursuit of butterflies, whose death in any case would be painless.

I suppose that it is the inexhaustible supply of certain insects, coupled with their absence of charm, which allows us to kill them so mercilessly. The Victorians used to test their own morality with this question: 'If you knew that by pressing a button here in England you could kill an unknown Chinaman in China, and by his death receive a million pounds, can you be sure that you would not do it?' The fact that the victim came from China, whose multitudes have always seemed both inexhaustible (though possibly they are not) and without charm for the Western world, made the test more severe. Among so many, and all looking so unattractively alike, how could one be missed? No doubt a Small White (perhaps I should say that I am speaking now of butterflies) is more destructive than a Clouded Yellow, but it is the comparative rarity and the greater beauty of the latter which protect it; just as it is the pretty shell-case of the ladybird which saves it from the repulsion and instant annihilation reserved for black insects of that size. Physical beauty and grace will take the animal world a long way—except, of course, among otter-hunters. But then otter-hunters are

> An idiot race, to honour lost;
> Who know them best, despise them most——

although, by some neglect, a recent correspondence in the Press on River Pollution made no mention of them.

In the language of the day it is customary to describe a certain sort of book as 'escapist' literature. As I understand it, the adjective implies, a little condescendingly, that the life therein depicted cannot be identified with the real life which the critic knows so well in W.C.1; and may even have the disastrous effect on the reader of taking him happily for a few hours out of his own real life in N.W.8. Why this should be a matter for regret I do not know; nor why realism in a novel is so much admired when realism in a picture is condemned as mere photography; nor, I might add, why drink and fornication should seem to bring the realist closer to real life than, say, golf and gardening.

However this be, the escapists make a brave show on our shelves. From the author of the *Iliad* to the author of *Hamlet*, from Defoe to Dumas, from Anthony Hope to Agatha Christie, they have all taken us out of our own experience into strange worlds. We can lose ourselves in Strelsau as in Elsinore, in Troy as on a desert island; fascinated we can watch the little grey cells at work of Belgian and of Dane. There is no need to be ashamed of the detective story which is so exciting that 'it is impossible to put it down once you have taken it up', merely to be smug about the four-generation chronicle which it is impossible to take up once you have put it down. Sometimes I think wistfully of a world in which the conventional literary values are transposed; a world in which romance is rated above realism, and comedy above tragedy; a world, to give an example, in which critics would not qualify so loftily Mr Calverley's little book of light verse, but keep their condescension for the mausoleum of heavy verse by a Mr Milton.

But not even the most relentless realist will grudge the escaping holiday-maker his escapist literature. He will have to take it with him; for hotels, boarding-houses and 'lodgings' are notoriously conservative about reading matter. In 1939, when I was going away for a golfing holiday, a kindly publisher presented me with the six latest detective stories by his and (henceforward) my favourite author; and being equally kind, or foolish, I left them behind in the hotel. But one cannot depend on this sort of thing, *The Mystery of a Hansom Cab* and *By Order of the Czar* being the seaside's more customary concession to modernity.

Generally speaking, and without reference to the Whiskey-

Straight school of America (in which the interest centres on
the number of drinks, blondes and beatings-up the 'Private
Eye' can absorb in a day's induction), the modern English
detective novel takes one of two forms. Chesterton said, and
I think truly, that the right and natural medium for a tale
of crime and detection was the short story. His feeling seems
to have been that, if a detective wanted 80,000 words in
which to solve a problem, he wasn't a very good detective,
and that in any case he couldn't be detecting all the time.
A detective novel, then, tends to become either a Short
Story Expanded or a Short Story Delayed. *The Moonstone*
is an outstanding example of the first sort. As a detective
story it could be told completely in 10,000 words. As a
romance, with a mysterious jewel and a mysterious theft in
it, and if nobody is in any hurry, it can be told in as many
words as you like. Wilkie Collins limited himself for some
reason to 200,000. I won't say that he couldn't have spared
one of them, but the total is extremely enjoyable. There are
those who think highly of Sergeant Cuff 'of the Detective
Police', famous for a love of roses which set the fashion for
so many side-lines of so many sleuths. I am not of his ad-
mirers. He failed to detect anything, although the identity of
the ostensible thief was written as clearly in every action of
the heroine as in the behaviour of the supposed accomplice.
He merely added a second mystery to the first: the mystery of
himself. Who and what was Cuff? Of nation-wide fame as
a detective, yet still only a sergeant; only a sergeant, yet on
terms of professional equality with the local Superintendent;
sent down to the scene of the crime by the Chief Commis-
sioner, yet accepting a cheque from the mistress of the house
for his services; he is the real, unsolved problem of the book.
    There are two versions of the Short Story Delayed. In

the simpler version we are with the corpse all the time.
('One of the barbituric group,' says the doctor, sniffing at
it.) Among the guests at the house-party, by some happy
accident, is the Gifted Amateur; hardly an amateur, however, because he is either the nephew of the Assistant Com-
missioner, or else helped the Inspector in the Wyke-Snodsby
case last September—see reference at bottom of page, in
case you care to make a note of it for your library list. He
is allowed, therefore, to take part in the interrogation of the
other guests, his part being confined to a single unrelated
question asked of each one; as it might be, 'Did you notice
if there was a light in the lavatory?' or 'Have you ever heard
Sir John mention Ashton-under-Lyne?' One begins to feel
a little sorry for the Inspector, so obviously out of his class,
who is still plodding along with such old-time stuff as 'When
did you last see the deceased?' and 'Was he in his usual
spirits?' Chapter by chapter the guests tell their story; the
inquest has been held; and our hero is now in a position to
mention casually that he knew who the murderer was three
days ago. Unfortunately (or fortunately) 'one little piece of
the jig-saw is still missing', and the Inspector is not surprised
to hear—or shouldn't be, if he remembers the Wyke-
Snodsby case as well as we do—that his colleague 'prefers
to keep his own counsel until his case is complete'; thus delay-
ing induction and deduction for another eight chapters while
everybody's alibi is traced. Then at last comes the Great
Elucidation. This is the sleuth's, and our, big moment, and
he is not going to leave anything out. 'You remember,' he
begins rather unnecessarily, 'how the body of Sir John was
found lying in the library on the morning of May 14th,'
and so goes on: the delayed short story for which the reader
has been waiting . . .

In the other version in this kind the delay is more deliberate. The author starts off with a straightforward novel in which everybody hates everybody else, and nobody is without a strong motive for murdering somebody. In this way the murder is postponed to p. 120, and we are kept pleasantly wondering who is to be the victim. Sir Roger, is it? —and we were hoping it would be Eustace. No matter; we can now match our own detective powers against those of Authority, professional or amateur.

Unfortunately this contest (which, to me is the chief attraction of the detective story) can never be a completely fair one. The fact that two of the suspects are in love with each other means little to Scotland Yard, but a great deal to us. Love affairs have no place in a detective story. They are not only a waste of time when one is on the scent, but they spoil the reader's run by giving him a shorter cut to the kill than either he desires, or, probably, the author realizes. It is not merely that hero and heroine are above suspicion, but that their immunity is apparently shared by all the blood-relations on both sides, a necessary precaution if the strain is to be kept pure when they marry and live happy ever after. This, though laudable from the eugenist's point of view, narrows the field of suspicion considerably, and throws an undue responsibility on the uncles and aunts by marriage. I read a story once in which a nice young girl lived on the scene of the crime with a disagreeable stepfather. I wondered why she did this, for she had money of her own, and no great love for him. Naturally, when she began to fall in love with the detective, I deduced that the stepfather was the murderer. This, of course, would not be so obvious to Scotland Yard; but to the well-trained inductive reader it explained at once why the author had avoided the more ordinary picture of a nice young girl living with her father.

Another advantage which we can claim derives from the Inspector's unawareness of the special inhibitions of his creator. To know beforehand that a Roman Catholic is safe from the rope in a Chesterton story; that no Labour Member will commit a murder for the sake of the Coles; that one can hardly expect Miss Dorothy Sayers to hang a real Oxford man: this gives us an unfair start on an inspector whose open mind only excludes suspicion of the local superintendent. Moreover, the clues in the case, which have an objective value for the detective, have an additional subjective value for the reader. Relevant information, as that the elder nephew inherits £100,000, presents itself equally to both; but the news, casually imparted, that the younger nephew won the Pole Jump at Cambridge, or has made his own wireless set, has an importance outside its intrinsic worth. Why should the author give us such irrelevant information, if it is not a relevant factor in the solution?

As against all this, the Inspector is only up against the murderer, whereas we are up against the author, whose command of the situation is much more decisive. After all, he is deliberately trying to deceive the reader; and though we tell ourselves complacently that he is only trying to deceive the average reader, he may still have his eye on us. No fair-minded author will let his detective say in the last chapter 'I happened to overhear Sir John asking the butler,' if we haven't overheard it too. He will give us all the clues, but these may point to more than one person, and the final decision is his. The Great Elucidation does not always establish the innocence of all but one, as convincingly as it establishes the guilt of one, and we are left unsatisfied; telling ourselves peevishly that our solution is the better one, and that if we had been on the jury . . .

Anybody who has served on a jury as often as I have is aware that the real horror of the law is the conviction of everyone concerned with it that the mental age of a juryman is five, and that things must be explained to the poor child carefully, slowly, repeatedly and at enormous length. Actually, of course, it is the social age of Judge and Counsel which is about five. In a case a few years ago one of the witnesses who had sent his love to his mother-in-law—('I'm writing to mother, dear. Any message?' 'Oh, give her my love')—was severely cross-examined on his hypocrisy, perjury and unexampled depravity as revealed by an admission in Court that, in fact, he had never much cared for his mother-in-law. The Judge weighed in on the same lines; and there seemed to be a general inability of anybody in a wig to understand that 'Love to Elsie and the dogs' is often sent without a preliminary plumbing of the depths of one's emotion. In fact, except when one of our Communists is writing to Stalin, it means no more than 'your humble, obedient servant'.

One reads of 'brilliant cross-examinations', but to the weary listener in the jury-box the brilliance never gets through. This is largely due to the interval between each question: an interval occupied by the Judge in writing down the last question and answer in a laborious long-hand, by the jury in forgetting what the previous question was, and by the witness in preparing himself for the next one; so that the next question when it comes is something of an anti-climax for all. No stage producer would stand for it. Even if the cross-examination went at a reasonable pace, I doubt if it would move a juryman to enthusiasm. Occasionally a witness, particularly if he comes from what used to be called condescendingly the lower orders and may still be called un-truthfully the working class, will bring a touch of real life into Court, but Judge and Counsel in their wigs remain aloof from humanity.

One of the less reasonable but more pardonable weak-nesses of the Englishman is his hearty dislike of any sort of official. I doubt if Counsel has ever endeared himself to the jury, to whom his eyes so often and so appealingly turn. In one of those motor-accident cases, which have taken honest men from their work more often than any other form of compulsion, a child of eight was suing, through her father, for compensation. She had some such name as Elsie Prender-gast, and her counsel, calling her Elsie, had asked her the few necessary questions. Counsel for the Defence rose to cross-examine. It was to be a gentle, a sympathetic cross-examination: one reassuring eye on Elsie, the other on the jury, asking for our admiration of his way with children.

'Well, Elsie,' he began, stopped a moment, flashed the message to us 'Now listen to this, this will make you laugh,' and said archly, 'Or shall I call you Miss Prendergast?'

Elsie swallowed, and said 'Miss Prendergast.' Counsel, who had expected to lead the laughter, followed it sheepishly, and for the rest of the cross-examination had to call her Miss Prendergast. Elsie loved it. She had never been called Miss Prendergast before. The jury also loved it. Counsel, who had so often made a witness look a fool, was now looking a fool himself. For the freedom enjoyed by Counsel is the freedom

enjoyed everywhere by the official. He is licensed to be as
mocking, as disingenuous, as insulting as he pleases, but any
retaliation by the witness is met by an instant plea for the
protection of the Court, and a stern reproof by the Judge.

But whatever the juryman may think of the Bar, he cannot deny that it is respectable. It is, in fact, the only respectable calling open to the socially ambitious mother. With her
boy at the Bar, she can look any other woman in the face.
The most outrageous, long-haired quack can call himself a
doctor; Mr Squeers and Mr Creakle were as surely schoolmasters as Dr Arnold; and though to be a clergyman meant
something once, if it were made quite clear that one was not
one of those impossible Nonconformists, the social standards
of the Church of England (alas! poor mother) are not what
they were. As for business and the arts, it is hopeless to expect
any re-assurance from them. To be described on the charge-
sheet (as one so often is) as 'engineer', 'author', 'actor' or
'financier' leaves one's social background uncertain, even
though one makes the headlines as an 'ex-public-schoolboy'
arrested at a 'West End Club'. But if one is a barrister, one
is 'at the Bar', and there is no more to be said. One is a
gentleman.

A rather uneasy gentleman sometimes, perhaps. Consider
the case of Seddon the poisoner. It was the opinion of
Marshall Hall, who defended him, that in Seddon he had
'plumbed the depths of human wickedness'. Seddon was 'as
wicked as a sane man could be'. Marshall Hall, defending him on the capital charge, gets up to cross-examine the
chief medical witness for the prosecution. Marshall Hall's
biographer, also a barrister, conducts us through the highly
technical cross-examination up to a certain point, and then
says:

Here, I think, Marshall Hall should have sat down. If he had, Seddon might well have gone free, and Marshall, by sheer scholarship and skill in using it, would have achieved a marvellous forensic triumph.

Now, outside the Temple one does not think of murder trials in terms of forensic triumphs. One passionately wants the innocent freed and the guilty condemned. In this trial Marshall Hall apparently knew, if not at the beginning of it, certainly at the end, that he was defending the wickedest murderer of his time. The police say, 'Once a poisoner, always a poisoner.' Did he regret afterwards that he did not sit down at the right moment, and thus enable Seddon to continue his experiments with arsenic? Did he weep over that missed forensic triumph? One does not know. Yet a profession in which at any moment one may have to rejoice as a citizen in one's failures and deplore as a gentleman one's successes is not altogether a comfortable profession.

It may be said, and doubtless is said, that Justice is best obtained by holding the balance between two extreme views of the case, each view maintained by a single-minded partisan. Possibly it is so. Possibly the best way to paint a door green is to put on first an exact shade of blue and then an exact shade of yellow. But this is a very different thing from giving one man, of a certain experience, energy, and artistry a blue paint-pot, and another man of other experience, energy and artistry a yellow paint-pot, and letting them both do their damnedest. Counsel for the prosecution, or the plaintiff, is not out to give the jury a certain conventional blue, but to make things look as blue as he can for the defendant, whose counsel in reply goes all over yellow. Occasionally, quite by accident, something recognizable as green may be achieved. But at other times . . .

For the Bar, however strenuously it denies it, is always on
the horns of this dilemma: that either Justice is continually
thwarted, or that forensic triumphs are only triumphs of the
imagination, and the 'princely fees' demanded for them are
demanded under false pretences. A layman naturally prefers
to think that Justice is independent of forensic triumphs;
that men's lives do not depend upon whether a particular
counsel is briefed, or being briefed, sits down at the right
moment. He has good reason for thinking so. For the last
word is with the jury, and the jury, dragged unwillingly from
its work or its leisure, and bitterly resenting the whole business, is the coldest audience possible for the costume play
which Judge and Counsel are putting on. So naïve, so much
of it.

The prisoner has gone into the witness-box and told his
story, denying or explaining away all the evidence which
the Prosecution has produced. Counsel rises dramatically to
cross-examine.

'I suggest,' he says, with the air of one making a good
point, 'that your whole story is a tissue of lies from beginning
to end.'

How surprised he would be if the prisoner coughed sheepishly, and said, 'Well, now you put it like that, Guv'nor, I
believe you're right.' But what, otherwise, is the point of the
suggestion? Suppose that instead of saying 'I suggest', he
had done what it is his business to do: asked the witness a
question.

'Is the whole story which you have just told the Court a
tissue of lies from beginning to end?'

It would be an idiotic question to ask, wouldn't it? But, in
fact, Counsel is not addressing the prisoner at all. He is
addressing the jury; though to what purpose remains a

mystery. The jury won't wake up suddenly, and tell themselves that at last they've got the idea, this chap is *against* the prisoner, he doesn't *believe* him! It will remain stolid.

So I shall now suggest that this silly 'I suggest' habit of Counsel's should in future be disbarred; that, until it is, witnesses should look at the ceiling, twiddle their thumbs, and coldly ignore all such personal confidences as Counsel feels called on to make; and that if the Judge says sternly, as he probably will, 'Answer the question, sir!' somebody should take him away, and explain very slowly to him the nature of a mark of interrogation.

Having said all this, I shall add that I have the honour to know a number of admirable gentlemen in various shaped wigs, that I respect them highly, and that, if ever I am arrested, I shall unhesitatingly put my case in the hands of the most forensically triumphant of them, and look to him for a good deliverance.

NOBODY who heard on that September morning in 1939 the doleful voice of Neville Chamberlain, announcing that we were now at war with Germany, will ever forget it. A few, a very few, of those who heard it may have foreseen that the war would last nearly six years. Not one of them would have believed it possible that within two years of the end of it the fear of a new and more terrible war would be overshadowing the world.

I have been an ardent Pacifist since 1910, and still am. In my vocabulary a Pacifist is not the same as a Conscientious Objector. Nothing is gained by burying one's head in the sand when war breaks out, and supposing that it will pass one by. On the contrary, as long as one is alive one is taking part in the war, willingly or unwillingly, actively or passively, as a force or as a deadweight: that is, one is helping either one's country or the enemy. The only logical protest for a Conscientious Objector who refuses to take part is suicide; preferably at sea, so that the war effort shall not be interrupted by the need for burying the body.

A Pacifist, in my definition, is one who does not believe that war is 'a legitimate extension of policy' or 'a biological necessity' or 'human nature', and who does believe that its economic gains are illusory. So, since it results in the torture and death of innocent and harmless people, he is not only of opinion that it should be outlawed, but looks forward to a day when the whole world will share his opinion. Common sense and common decency, he tells himself, must surely prevail.

In 1910 Pacifism was derided. All the wars in the memory of Englishmen had taken place outside their country, and could be followed with the eager but impersonal interest with which we now follow the broadcast of a cricket match. It was true that a few soldiers got killed, but this was just an occupational risk, cheerfully to be accepted in return for the adventure and the glory promised. If the civilians did think about war in the abstract, they told themselves that it was bracing, like corporal punishment and cold baths; and that, since it had been going on for thousands of years, it would probably be wrong, and would certainly be impossible, to stop it now. So Pacifists were dismissed as idealists, cranks, and, as likely as not, vegetarians.

In 1920 nearly everybody in this country was a Pacifist in theory, and millions of them were Pacifists in practice: that is, they were trying and hoping, by means of the League of Nations, to make an end of war. This change of opinion was due, and due only, to the experience of a war much more terrible than any that they had known, and much nearer home; a war which had cast its shadow over nearly every family in the land.

By 1945 Pacifism was the accepted policy of the whole country. This was because, and only because, the destruction of so many lives, of so much beauty, in our own fortress, had blasted, for all and for ever, the old conventional beliefs.

But there were still a few in the world who believed that

war could be used profitably for their own purposes. They
were not to be found among the common people; nor in
those countries whose Governments were chosen by the
common people; but only in those countries where the common people are oppressed and silent, and where a few fools,
a few criminals, can still falsify the conclusions of humanity.
Fortunately for the rest of the world humanity now has the
atom bomb, and on the subject of war the atom bomb will
speak the last word.

The atom bomb is the final proof of what Norman Angell
called the Great Illusion. He proved to the conviction of some
of us in 1910—a conviction which two World Wars have so
enormously sustained and enlarged—the simple truth that a
victorious war brings in no material dividends. This did not
prove, of course, that there was nothing to be won by an
aggressive war; for there are other gains in a Dictator's mind
than economic ones. But all the aesthetic pleasure of a triumphal victory march across Europe, Hammer and Sickle
waving with the cohorts in the van, and Grand Inquisitors
trotting up behind with the baggage-train, would be lost in
the knowledge that there was no Moscow to return to, no
Kremlin to give orders to its new puppets. Not only Moscow, not only the Kremlin would be gone, but the whole
political structure which has kept the Russian people in
slavery would be disrupted. Whatever illusion of victorious
gain wars of the past may have presented to power-drunk
autocrats, it is visible now, even to the fool and the criminal,
that nothing is to be gained by a deliberately provoked
atomic war.

Shortly before he died in 1895 Louis Pasteur was asked if
he could see any way by which war could be abolished. He
replied that there was only one way, but that this way was

certain. War would abolish itself. It would become so devastating that it would become impossible. No doubt he was thinking of bacteriological war, but atomic war has got there first. It is because, and only because, the Kremlin sees no credit balance in an atomic war that it is so desperately anxious to ban the atom bomb. It wants to get back to the old kind of war, for which it has in full measure the material, the will, and the illusion of profit. It is peace from the determent of the atom bomb which is the sole object of its Peace Crusade. The strategics of the atom bomb are not that bombs in one place make up for a deficiency of tanks in another; nor that we are only safe so long as we have a superiority in them of x to one; nor that it is a retaliatory weapon as gas was in the last war, only to be used if the other side uses it first. The atom bomb is a weapon, not for victory in war, not for 'pairing' with the enemy in war, but to prevent war. To be prepared so to use it demands courage: the courage Samson showed when he pulled down the pillars of the temple. Samson sacrificed himself. By making it perfectly clear now that the next war will be an atomic war: that, without regard to the atom bombs Russia may have, or her intention, or lack of intention, to use them, at the first movement of Communist troops against any country in the West, Moscow will be wiped out: we shall take the risk of sacrificing ourselves. It is a small risk compared with the certainty of war otherwise; a cheaply-bought risk for those of us who would far sooner die under an atom bomb than live under the Kremlin.

Unfortunately there are many good people, both in Britain and, more importantly, in America, who cannot bring themselves to accept the atom bomb as within the limits of what they call 'legitimate warfare'. Perhaps because I became a

Pacifist on impersonal grounds, before I had experienced the horrors or even the discomforts of war, I consider all war, from the wars of the Israelites onwards, to be horrible, and all weapons of war, from the sword and the club and the spear onwards, to be barbarous. Every distinction between weapons of war as legitimate and illegitimate, as acceptable by, or repugnant to, humanity, is one more admission that war itself is acceptable and legitimate, so long as it is conducted in some fashion hallowed by previous exercise. If war is to be abolished, it will not be abolished by pretending that one method of killing is pleasing to God, and another displeasing; by accepting gratefully 200 raids with ordinary bombs which kill 1,000 'civilians' apiece, and exhibiting sanctimonious horror at one raid with an atomic bomb which kills the same number of 'civilians', and spares 20,000 airmen's lives.

I put the civilians into inverted commas to show that they have not yet got into uniform. I have never understood why the death of a clerk, a ploughman or a poet calls for a greater compassion from man, and a severer condemnation from God, if he should still be wearing his ordinary clothes. The object of aggressive war (however wrong) is to impose the national will upon another nation by the destruction of so much of its resources, human and material, that it can defend itself no longer. The object of defensive war (however right) is to resist that imposition by an even greater destruction of the enemy's resources, human and material. The human resources of a nation are every man, woman and child belonging to it. Yes, even children. Children in 1939 were young men and women in 1945, serving their country.

For war is hell, and it is not possible to contract out of all responsibility for hell by a high-minded disapproval of one particular mode of torture; nor would it be edifying to single out for disapproval the mode which particularly threatened oneself. A conscience which is outraged by the atom bomb should have been outraged long ago by war; for war has never made careful selection of its victims, nor been restrained by their number. A war to resist Communism would not be a game to be played under arbitrary rules, with certain approved weapons of a carefully limited range of destruction; it would be a life-and-death struggle, in which the West would only be engaged because it believed that there were higher values at stake than human lives.

Even the lives of its last man, woman and child. Even the lives of the enemy.

The train was speeding across the North American continent from Idaho to Wyoming, with Three-fingered Al on board. He had shot his man in Idaho, and was fleeing to Wyoming, where it wouldn't matter so much. This was either because they executed you in a less unpleasant way in Wyoming; or because there was no extradition from there; or because, in any case, there would be certain formalities to be gone through before the criminal was handed over, which would delay Justice for an extra two or three years while Al was holding his Press Conferences. Or, possibly, because I have got the names of the States wrong, and they were two other States. All we need to know is that while the train was in motion, and the landscape was scurrying past the window, Al was in danger; as soon as the train stopped across the border, he was safe. Dramatic.

For, as you have guessed, the Idaho police were on board too. Like Al they had a compartment to themselves, in which they slapped their holsters, chewed gum and assured each other that the sonofabitch was undoubtedly among those present. But though they looked into every compartment but the one in which Al sat alone, they could not find him. It is possible, of course, that they did not know him by sight.

So the train rushed on, carrying Al and the police and, it was hoped, the public with it: the police relentlessly chewing gum and searching in the wrong places, Al chewing his under-lip and casting nervous glances at the corridor. And as the scene flashed from one protagonist to the other without bringing them very much closer, somebody on the executive must have said to his fellow-thinkers, 'Is this enough? Can we go on like this until we reach Wyoming? What—to consider only one class of the community—what of the Mothers? Are we doing enough for *them*? True, we are giving them, as Aristotle so clearly put it, the imitation of an action that is serious and also complete in itself, with incidents arousing pity and terror, wherewith to accomplish its purgation of such emotions. But what of the lump in the throat, the rush of unbidden tears to the bridge of the nose, such as is best engendered by the unexpected appearance of a little child? A child, gentlemen, an innocent female child, plunged into the underworld of crime.'

I do not say that these were his actual words, but the thought behind them was there. It went over well. So now, once more, we are watching Al registering the emotions proper to one in his position, or, like him, admiring so much of Idaho as flashes past the window . . . when suddenly our attention is diverted to the corridor. What do we see? We see an india-rubber ball bouncing along, dropped maybe from a child's idle fingers. Where is it going? The more alert-minded of us have guessed. It swerves to the right and dis-appears into Al's compartment. The child and we follow.

It is easy to imagine Al's emotions. It is easier, however, to watch them running over his face: the panic at the entrance of the unknown; the relief at seeing only a child; the annoy-ance at the interruption to his thoughts; the realization that perhaps he himself was a child once, before he became a gun-man. All this we see, as she recovers her ball and sits herself next to him. Holding out a book to him, she says 'Will 'oo wead to me?'

Does some thought of his own childhood (if any) suddenly overwhelm him? Does a strange new upsurging of kindness rise in his heart as he takes the book in his hand? Or is it his hope that, seeing him thus engaged, any Police Captain who has not wasted his pay at the pictures will look elsewhere now for his suspect? We shall never know. A firm distinction be-tween these emotions is too much for one face to express. We can see that he reads unwillingly, but this may be because he can only just read.

He opens the book at random, and stumbles through the lines. What is he reading? *'Jack and Jill went up the hill . . .'* *'And the Big Bear said " Who's been eating MY porridge?" . . .'* *'Once upon a time there was a King . . .'* Does it matter? It does not matter. He has, it may be, an Idahoan accent; being a gunman, he is compelled by his Trade Union to speak out of the side of his mouth; he is a man of small vocabulary, and many of the words are strange to him. In any case the mother will be here directly, putting her pretty head in at the door, and saying, 'I do hope my little girl has not been a nuisance, come along, darling,' and the scene will be over. Was he reading *Mother Goose*, or *Cinderella*, or *The Jumblies*? Before an expert could decide, the book would be closed, and the child bedward. Does it matter what he reads?

Indeed it does. For this is where I step into the picture, to my own great profit. The book was mine. Don't ask me why a Film Corporation should pay 750 dollars for the right to use four lines from a copyright book, when it has volumes of better, non-copyright work available, for which it need not pay anything. Don't ask me why, having so paid, it should choose the least-known, least-quoted, least-typical poem of the forty-four in the book: a poem, called apparently 'Pinkle Poyer', about a kitten. Don't ask me, because you know the answer yourself. It is just what Film Corporations do. Long may they go on doing it.

It is not often that a writer says of another's work 'I wish I had written that.' Writers, like all other men and women, cling to their own personalities. A pleasantly illiterate young man who says 'I wish I was Hutton' means 'I wish I could play cricket like Hutton', which would give him no more than an added grace to his own delightful self. But if he were to say 'I wish I could write books like Hemingway,' he would be saying, though he might not know it, 'I wish I were Hemingway,' and would be himself no longer.

For this reason a writer will admire the work of another writer without wishing that he had written it; knowing that, being what he is, he never could have written it, and that being somebody else, he would have lost all that he had himself written. So I have never said to myself 'I wish that I had written *Hamlet*,' and with Hamlet go a great many other plays and books whose authors I reverence. But there are works, particularly works of humour, which are more impersonal, being built on a happy idea, such as might come to another, and sustained with a scholarship or craftsmanship which oneself might have acquired without losing one's identity. In my vain solicitude for the masterpieces which I did not write, I limit myself to desire for those which might have appeared over my name without being immediately attributed to a contemporary Bacon for whom I was standing in. Critics would say, very properly, that I had surpassed myself, and that none of my earlier work had led them to suppose that I was capable of this; but they would accept the fact that writers do sometimes surpass themselves, and that the most unlikely might bring off a masterpiece one day, as it were, by accident.

Assuming, then, that they had not been written already, I should die happy if I could write one more book and one more play. The book would be *The Private Life of Helen of Troy* and the play *The Importance of Being Earnest*. For these my admiration is profound. Many years ago I used to subscribe to an American press-cutting agency; but after receiving 153 notices of *The Late Christopher Bean*, I withdrew my subscription, fearing that future references to Sir Christopher Wren might prove a still more irresistible attraction to the clipper. More lately my name found itself to its pride among the select and brilliant few who write *The Times* 'fourth leaders'. These undeserved tributes come to one from time to time, sometimes in reverse. I sat next to a woman painter at dinner once, and she asked me who I was and what I did. Pursuing the matter laboriously at her request, we looked about for a book or play which would identify me a little more clearly; but without success until I mentioned *Mr Pim Passes By*. This rang the bell. 'Oh, I know that,' she said. 'But I always thought H. G. Wells wrote it.' It would be a red-letter day for me, should a painter or a press-clipper think for one wild moment that I had written *The Private Life of Helen of Troy* or *The Importance of Being Earnest*.

The last two acts of *The Importance of Being Earnest* are set in The Manor House, Woolton, Hertfordshire, the country home of Mr John Worthing. For the encouragement of British Railways I propose to examine the train service which the village of Woolton enjoyed in 1894 under private enterprise.

The first arrival from London on this July afternoon is Algernon Moncrieff, nephew of Lady Bracknell. Internal evidence allows us to put the time at 3.30. He is followed by John Worthing, who arrives about seven minutes later (3.37); by the Hon. Gwendolen Fairfax (3.58); and by her mother, Lady Bracknell (4.28). Since each of these four was related to, or an old friend of, the others, and was greatly surprised by their arrival, it is clear that they came by different trains. Lady Bracknell, indeed, announces that she followed her daughter 'at once by a luggage train'. This seems a little capricious of her. With three passenger trains arriving within half an hour, it is unlikely that she would have had long to wait for a fourth. As it is, we can but admire the unusual speed of the G.N.R.'s goods service, and the elasticity which allowed her ladyship to travel by it.

Now three Down trains and a goods train arriving at a
small country station within the hour is well enough; though
not enough, perhaps, to impress any but the regular users of
small country stations. But we must remember that other
trains may have been flowing in at short intervals conveying
other passengers than those destined for The Manor House.
Indeed, to judge from the Up service, they must have been
pouring in. At about 4.35 Lady Bracknell looks at her watch
and says 'Gwendolen, the time approaches for our departure.'
A little before 4.45 she looks at her watch again, and says
'Come, dear, we have already missed five, if not six, trains.'
Even accepting the lower estimate we can still admire the
almost reckless enthusiasm of the Great Northern Railway.
Today my own country station offers nothing between 3.13
and 5.14. However, as the 3.13 takes just over three hours to
cover 36¾ miles, and the 5.14 just under two hours, it is
perhaps as well that we are exposed to no further temptation.

It is, I suppose, possible that some dogged Public Relations
Officer, wishing to do what he can for nationalization, will
now point out that *The Importance of Being Earnest* is a work
of the imagination, and that the train service to an imaginary
village in it cannot legitimately be compared with that provided so efficiently by British Railways. If so (and it would
be very unromantic of him) he will merely shunt me on to
another line. I shall now invite the innocent public, which
knows so little and cares so little about the troubles of a
writer, to consider how the passing years have removed, or
added to, those troubles.

Wilde wanted to get four people from London to The
Manor House, Woolton, so that they arrived at four different
times between 3.30 and 4.30. There was only one way of
bringing them there—by train. Had this been what is called

a serious play, he would have been criticized severely for his
indifferent craftsmanship and his poor sense of reality. Today,
how easy! Any character can arrive anywhere at any time,
dependent only on his own whim and that of the author.
Any number of people can start from London at the same
time, if that be necessary to the plot, and arrive as required at
any Manor House in any county. They can start at different
times, and enter, should the situation demand it, dramatically
together. They have driven down, and the horse-power of
their cars, or the speed-lust of the drivers, is of no moment to
anybody. No explanations are asked for or expected. Add to
the motor-car the telephone, and the modern dramatist is
seen to be on velvet, or in clover, whichever he prefers.

LADY MARY (*in the middle of triangular drama*): I think it
would be as well if my solicitor were here. He lives at the
other end of the Cromwell Road, but he has a fast car. If
you will excuse me, Mrs Fortescue, I will ring him up.

(*She goes out, thus giving George and Mrs Fortescue the short,
passionate love-scene which the audience was beginning to wonder
if it would get. Without the bites it would look nothing in print,
and we shall therefore leave it out. Lady Mary returns.*)

GEORGE: Is he coming?

LADY MARY: By a fortunate chance, he had only just
reached home, so that his car was already at the door. He will
be here at any moment. (*A bell rings.*) Ah, there he is.

You see how easy it is, and why so many good plays keep
coming on. (And, of course, off.)

But don't suppose that the modern writer has it all his own
way. Whether in novel or play, he has to surmount a difficulty which never confronted the Victorian. I think it is true
to say that in the 35 years between 1860 and 1895 nothing

happened in England which mattered to the creative writer. This meant that he was not compelled to date his novel or his play. The Time could be roughly, and need not be accurately, The Present. If ten years elapsed before his play was accepted, it would make no difference. The Time could still be The Present.

The modern author cannot ignore time like this. In the 35 years between 1914 and 1949 there is no vague Present Time. Things happened, people were born, lived or died during the First World War, between the two wars, during the Second World War, or during the Great Peace. It is not merely that a play written in 1939 with footmen in it, and accepted in 1949, must be either a costume play ('Time, 1938'), or else sacrifice its footmen; and with them, possibly, its more humorous situations. If that were all, one could write another play and hope that this time the manager would manage to read it more quickly. The trouble is that, with the exception of the very old and the very young, every man and woman has taken some part in public events. Jane Austen, writing through the Napoleonic Wars, could, and quite rightly did, ignore them. As an artist she preferred to leave them out, and as an artist she wrote of people who, in fact, did leave them out. Modern wars, and, apparently, modern peace, cannot be left out.

Now this may not seem to matter very much, but in fact it matters a great deal. While he is writing, a novelist is a god, master of his creatures. Drawing on his personal memories, his observation and his imagination, he creates his private world, in which his men and women show by thought, word and action as much of themselves as will bring them within his design. History, of course, is always there. Governments rise and fall: famous men live and die:

there are earthquakes in Italy, floods in China, and a Great
Exhibition in 1851. If the novelist is dating his story precisely,
he may, if he wish, include these, or any other, current
events; if he prefers not to date it, then, since the develop-
ment of his characters need not exhibit an awareness of them,
he can pass them by. His people live in their own world, a
world which may be just as real as the real world, but a
world in which the novelist is as much master of their circumstances as of themselves. They may live through 1851, and
give no public heed to the Great Exhibition: they may live
through 1861, and fail to comment on the death of the
Prince Consort: they can live through History up to 1914
. . . and never once will the reader be forced to wonder, or
the author to have decided, whether the Reform Bill had
been passed, Paris had been invested, or the first ha'penny
paper had been published.

But all this is changed. Today a novelist's characters are
circumscribed by History. Two World Wars and a Nether-
world Peace have played, and are still playing, a part in their
lives which cannot be ignored if they are to have any reality.
As his book runs through the years, the author will continually have to ask himself, 'Where am I now? What year is
this?' wondering whether the War is on, whether London is
being bombed, whether there is any petrol, and who does the
washing up. And, when, reluctantly, he has fixed his dates,
and so answered all his questions, then memory and observation, imaginatively rendered, must always be referred to his
time-sheet for confirmation. The dinner à deux which he
describes, remembering the first time he took his own girl to
the Savoy: the domestic difficulties of his newly-married
couple, based on remembered observation of some earlier
married life: whatever he writes can no longer flow freely

from his pen, leaving him blissfully indifferent to its source; it must all be considered, checked, and translated to its destined time. In short, little as he may like it, he is now writing an Historical Novel. He is no longer a master of circumstances. He is no longer a god.

When, as a very young man, I first saw him across the footlights, he was middle-aged, but already an old-fashioned actor. He had an orotund voice, and movements which matched it. One of the things about him which impressed me was the way he looked at his watch, preparatory to delivering some such line as 'Eleven fifteen, he should be here directly.' He made a ritual of it, loving every moment. Both hands to the left waistcoat pocket, the little finger of the right hand under the gold albert chain, a flick, and the gold hunter is within the palm of the left hand; a slight pause, and click! the lid flies open. The time is now available. But much remains to be done. The cupped hands are moved backwards and forwards with a slight, almost imperceptible motion, as of one playing a fish; then, the watch at last in focus, they come to rest. Cognition of the time sweeps slowly across the mobile face: a little raising of the eyebrows, a trifling awareness from the nostrils, indicating surprise that it is so late: and, as the watch is snapped shut and lowered gently with both hands into the waistcoat pocket, the words on which so much depends are delivered: 'Eleven fifteen! He should be here directly!'

Ten years later I joined his club, and got to know him

personally. Whatever I had thought of his acting, I soon came to know, as every old member knew, that he was one of the kindest and most delightful of men. Ours was only a club acquaintance, but as everybody called him Bertie, it seemed natural so to call him too. One day near the end of his time, when he was almost old enough to be my grandfather, even if he hadn't been before, he was coming from the hats-and-coats just as I was preparing to leave the club. With rather trembling hands he took my coat from its peg, and held it out for me. I said, a little ashamed that I had been slow enough to allow it, 'Oh no, Bertie, you really mustn't!'

And then, without hesitation and without mockery, he dropped the prettiest compliment. It was, of course, like so much that actors say, *vox et praeteria nihil*; to no man could he have meant it less, from no man could I have believed it less. But it was the perfect exit-line with which to leave me for the lounge, delivered with the charming, old-fashioned courtesy of his heyday. Was it his own, or was he quoting from some Victorian comedy? Wilde might have said it, but did not. Who then? for one feels that it cannot have been left unsaid for so long.

'Oh no, Bertie, you really mustn't.'

'My dear Milne, every man is a valet to his hero.'

I saw old Autumn in the misty morn
Stand shadowless like Silence, listening
To Silence.

Kipling (or a character in one of his stories) said that there were just five transcendent lines of enchantment in poetry; lines giving what Quiller-Couch called the Great Thrill. Two of these are known to everybody:

Charmed magic casements opening on the foam
Of perilous seas in faery lands forlorn.

The other three, not, perhaps, quite so well known, are

A savage place, as holy and enchanted,
As ever 'neath a waning moon was haunted
By woman wailing for her demon lover.

On my own account I add to them the lines with which I began, together with those earlier ones from *Kubla Khan*:

Where Alph the sacred river ran
Through caverns measureless to man
Down to a sunless sea.

and

While Ilion like a mist rose into towers.

If these five passages have anything in common, what is it?

166

I think it is that they transport us immediately into an experience which we seem to have known, in fact or in imagination, all our lives. They form, not only a picture in our minds, but a picture which, at the first reading of the lines, we felt had always been with us. The opening of Hood's *Ode to Autumn* is, perhaps, the least magical because we know that we have been there in fact; but I include it with the others because these give just the same immediate certainty of knowledge, and yet add to autumn their own magical air of unreality. Often I have told myself that I have experienced just that feel of silence on many an October day; but, as often, I have seen Ilion like a mist rise into towers: have been myself within that savage place, ringed with stone, watching and waiting: have reached the sunless sea. Which is truth?

Is it also part of this magic in poetry that the words used have an intensity beyond their meaning or their music? 'Shadowless': it means so little, and that little so obvious. How could a misty morn not be shadowless? But here it helps to create the slight air of apprehension that anything might happen, which one has felt sometimes in the stillness of autumn; almost as though the word were 'shadowing', and one were being followed. So, too, with 'sunless', sounding here so much more awful than it is. And has not 'perilous' a new meaning? Not 'dangerous'; not a stormy sea, with a gale blowing in at the windows, and the nightingale, somewhere at the back of the house, unheard; but midway between 'parlous' and 'pearly': an opalescent sea breaking gently into foam beneath the casements, but offering ventures for the venturesome in distant lands. The actual words seem to be but the scaffolding, no longer there when the whole beautiful structure is complete.

We are told to verify our quotations. This is particularly
necessary when claiming that we will 'never forget', or that
'everybody remembers', the 'immortal words' of So-and-so.
In an earlier chapter I quoted from the Bible, and referred my
memory of the lines to *The Oxford Dictionary of Quotations*,
this being within the easiest reach. There I found the most
shocking misprint of all time; one to make any writer
shudder, thinking 'It might have happened to me!'

The misprints which have become historical are not the
ones which really matter. They are only remembered because in the result they were funny, or libellous or improper.
The pressman who wrote 'the battle-scarred veteran', and
saw it printed 'the bottle-scarred veteran', was, one imagines,
merely amused; and still more amused when his apologetic
correction was misprinted 'battle-scared'. The misprints
which matter to a writer are those which miss the whole
point of what he meant to say, and yet so nearly say it that
they will never be recognized as misprints.

For instance: describing a return to the trenches in the
First War, after the usual four days out of the line, I wrote
that the dug-out cat had kittened in our absence, and went on
'However, as all the rats seem to have rottened, the position
is much the same.' A tiny joke, but, as they say, a joke is a
joke, and the printer snatched it from me by saying that the
rats had rattened. I had a similar experience, shared, I am sure,
with many dramatists, on the first night of a play. An Englishman, posing as a prince of an imaginary Balkan State, is

being questioned about his country by his fellow-guests for the evening, most of them snobbishly excited to be meeting 'Royalty'. Somebody says: 'Suppose we begin like the geography books. Chief industries. Exports and Imports.' He answers: 'Since the Peace Conference our chief industry has been fighting. If we declare war first, we export soldiers. If the enemy declares war first, we import them.' The actor, not being too sure of his words, said: 'If we declare war first, we import soldiers. If the enemy declares war first, we export them.' The audience vaguely felt that it was meant to be smart and wasn't. Well, what could one do about that? Nothing.

And now, not to keep the Editor of *The Oxford Dictionary of Quotations* in agony any longer, I shall reveal his horrid misprint.

In *Genesis* you will read these beautiful words:

And Jacob served seven years for Rachel; and they seemed unto him but a few days, for the love he had to her.

And in *The Dictionary of Quotations* you will read:

And Jacob served seven years for Rachel; and they seemed unto him but a few years, for the love he had to her.

All that beauty gone with one word! A living author so treated in the first printing of his book would feel that he could never write again. He would go straight off to the Rocky Mountains and shoot editors.

One constant difficulty which faces modest people like you, dear reader, and me is the difficulty of getting ourselves rightly appreciated. The genius, the saintliness, the high courage, the generosity, the—I am trying to work down to you —the ability to stand on the head or to recite the alphabet backwards: awareness of these gifts of ours should be the common property of mankind. Unfortunately mankind remains unaware.

What, then, are we to do? How can we get the knowledge across to the world, when modesty forbids us to be frank about ourselves or to employ a press agent, and when unsought occasions are too few to bring out all the wealth of character, parlour-tricks and anecdote which is stored within us? Must we rely entirely on chance to come to our aid? At first sight it would seem so.

Chance, unfortunately, takes her own time, as is shown by the well-known story of the old lady and the snake-charmer. She and her husband, a charming elderly couple, went to a local *fête* in support of somebody or something; whether of the Conservative candidate, who was just putting up for the constituency, or the church tower, which was just falling down in it, did not greatly concern any but the organizers. One of the attractions was an Indian snake-charmer's tent. It so happened that at the moment when all the snakes had come out of their box to gather round the snake-charmer and sway to his pipings, he was overcome by illness, dropped his pipe, and fell back unconscious. The snakes, no longer under control, and looking elsewhere for amusement, started a panic among the spectators; but before the children could be thoroughly trampled underfoot, the old lady stepped forward, took up the pipe, sat cross-legged on the ground, and gave the snakes the music which they loved. They hurried back to listen, rapt; and one by one she picked them up and returned them to their box.

As she and her husband were leaving the tent, followed by an enthusiastic and now intrepid crowd, he said to her:

'Why, Mary darling, we have known each other for more than fifty years, and you never told me you could charm snakes!'

And the old lady said: 'You never asked me, John.'

It is a pathetic story. Sometimes I have pictured to myself Mary's married life, waiting for all those years for a chance question from her husband. The revelation of her talent must have been so close so often. Perhaps, after no more than thirty years of wedded bliss, he picks up his paper one morning at breakfast, and reads of the arrival at the Zoo of a new snake, the deadly samba-samba of the East Macaroons. How easy for him to say humorously, 'What would you do, Mary, if you suddenly met a samba-samba?' How natural for her to answer, 'Darling, didn't I ever tell you, I used to be a snake-charmer.' But no. Once more he lets the occasion pass, merely asking why they *always* have the wrong sort of marmalade. . . .

Yet Mary was lucky in the end, for when the chance came to exhibit her talent, she was able to exhibit it to the full. In a different connexion I was once less fortunate.

Although my charm is rightly considered too elusive for snakes, among my own kind it can carry me to the end of a good story, given the right opening. Many years ago I wrote an article in which I happened to mention the inland resort of Hayes. As only the Hayes-conscious know, there is a Hayes in Middlesex, and a Hayes in Kent. A man who lived in the Hayes in Middlesex, and thought that I was referring to the Hayes in Kent, whereas I was referring to a Hayes which I supposed to be in Surrey, well, this man . . . well . . . well, it was a long time ago, and I really forget now what it was all about; but it did make an extremely funny story. Naturally it was a little egotistic at the start, involving, as it did, not only a certain amount of apparently pointless autobiography, but extracts of rather a dull nature from the article itself. The surprising and hilarious *dénouement*, however, more than made up for this, as would be clear, even now, if only I could remember it.

Well, there I was, with this delightful story in my head, waiting for an opportunity to share it with the world. A less modest man would have made his own opportunity, interrupting a discussion on the Boat Race with 'Mortlake, let me see, isn't that somewhere near Hayes? Talking of Hayes——' But, like Mary, I would not force the opening, but waited hopefully for it to present itself. As the months went by, I became less and less hopeful. Many people will have noticed, whether at christenings, weddings or funerals, how rarely the company finds itself talking about Hayes. One goes everywhere, one meets everybody, conversation ranges lightly from this subject to that, but in the matter of Hayes there is what can only be described as a conspiracy of silence. So it was now.

And then suddenly the opening came. These were the days when one paid Sunday calls in a top-hat, in return for hospitality received. I was so calling; and on my arrival I had found in the drawing-room my hostess, her lovely daughter Hildegarde (with whom at the time I was deeply in love), some sort of young female cousin, and an elderly man in whiskers. Balancing a slice of cake in a saucer, and a cup and saucer on the knee, we made idle conversation. And then the miracle happened. Casually, as if it were a matter of no moment at all, the owner of the whiskers said that he had to go to a place called Hayes next day, and did anybody know where it was.

At last! I swallowed the contemporary piece of cake, and prepared for action.

The mother said wasn't it in Surrey.

The cousin said oh, no, it was in Kent surely.

The daughter—(really, I might have written the dialogue myself)—the daughter turned to me with what I hoped was a loving smile, and said, 'Come on, which is it? I'm sure *you* can tell us.'

I said: 'Well, as a matter of fact, I can. There are two; one in Kent and one in Middlesex.'

'However do you know that?' asked the mother, wondering what sort of a son-in-law so knowledgeable a young man would make.

I gave the little laugh which I had prepared for the occasion (how many months ago!) and said: 'Well, it was rather funny. You see——'

I have already admitted that the preparatory groundwork of this story was dull. Indeed, as I ploughed through it, some of the eyes of my listeners became a little glazed. However, I got to the end of it at last, much to my own, and doubtless their, relief. Now for the side-splitting, delicious climax. I paused dramatically; I took a sip of tea; I said—

No, it was the footman who said it. He flung open the door and said, 'Sir John and Lady Push, Dr and Mrs Wotherspoon, Miss Tootle!' We all rose, leaving the story on the floor. We re-distributed ourselves. Ten subsequent minutes on the sofa with Miss Tootle, instructive as it was, did not compensate for the knowledge that I had lost my Hildegarde. For now she would never hear the end of the story . . . and would always suppose that she had . . .

Leaving Hayes for good, let us now consider what is the best agency for the untold story, the unrevealed talent, the insufficiently exposed character. The answer, and it may come as a shock to some, is Marriage.

JANE (*suddenly across the room to her husband, à propos of nothing*): Oh, Herbert, do tell them that story of the Soviet Commissar! (*To the company:*) A lovely story Herbert brought back from the Foreign Office. I simply screamed!

HERBERT (*surprised, or looking it*): Do you mean the one about——

JANE: Yes, that's the one!

HERBERT (*modestly to his neighbour*): It's just a story I heard (*looking round the room*)—I expect some of you know it—(*raising his voice*) about an American in Moscow. (*Settling down to it:*) Well, this fellow . . .

And there he is. But in Jane's house the motto is 'Equal pay for equal work'. So a little later:

HERBERT: By the way, Mrs Pentstemon, have you seen Jane's bedspread?

MRS PENTSTEMON: No. What's that?

JANE (*hearing from the other end of the room, and laughing a little too loudly*): Oh, Herbert, don't be such an idiot! As if Mrs Pentstemon could possibly want to see it! (*To her neighbour:*) How are your zinnias doing? Ours have been——

MRS P.: No, but I'm most interested. What is it? A bedspread?

HERBERT: Patchwork. She made it herself. It's really lovely.

JANE (*coming to them*): It's just a patchwork bedspread. They're rather fun to do, don't you think?

MRS P. (*getting up*): Oh, do show me. I adore patchwork, I should love to see it.

JANE: Oh, well, if you really want to. Only I warn you . . . (*They go upstairs.*)

And there she is.

It is supposed by some that this explains why such extremely odd-looking people get married. But, like so many other things, marriage is not fool-proof. There was once a wife (subsequently divorced) who followed up her husband's delightful story of an Englishman, a Scotsman and an Irishman with, 'Now tell them your *other* story, dear'; and there was the husband (now living alone) who said, 'Susan, you *must* show Mrs Gumbleton your wonderful way of bottling artichokes', when it was Mrs Gumbleton who had shown Susan.

In the case of the unmarried—and, after what I have just said, there may be some who prefer to remain so—the only possible ally is the Postman. Two methods present themselves:

1. *The Anonymous Letter* (such as was written by young Sebastian Popp to the Secretary of the exclusive club to which he aspired).

DEAR SIR,

If the Sebastian Popp now, as I hear, up for election to your club is the S. Popp of Popp and Co., Publishers, who dived off Waterloo Bridge to save my aunt's life in 1947, I feel it my duty to warn you against him. Being one of the six best shots in the country and a keen rider to hounds, he takes a sadistic delight in killing our harmless dumb friends regardless of their feelings. Yours faithfully,

LOVER OF ANIMALS.

We elected him at once.

2. *The Misaddressed Letter*. (This was accidentally enclosed in the wrong envelope and sent to Miss Lavinia Withers, the chief gossip in our neighbourhood.)

DEAR MONTY,

Yes, it is a long time since we climbed the Matterhorn together, and I was glad to hear from you again, and to learn that all your differences with the Americans were now settled. It was 255, not 256, that I made in that match against the M.C.C., fancy your remembering it! No, I haven't seen Winston lately, not since that day at Balmoral. Well——

Well, we can go on for as long as we like, and if Miss Withers is as trustworthy as she used to be, our local reputation, at least, will be assured; a reputation of which modesty will be one of the most endearing assets. '*Why*,' people will say, 'didn't he tell us himself?'

Like Hood and Keats (yet not like Hood and Keats) I, too, have written my *Ode to Autumn*: a literary event which modesty forbade me to mention in its more appropriate place at the beginning of this chapter. I began it just fifty years ago; so nobody will be surprised—or, of course, sorry —to hear that I remember only the last verse.

The general air of this ode, as I recall it, was one of desolation. The eager expectation of spring, the full ripeness of summer, all were gone; there was nothing to look forward to, nothing to enjoy. Youth was no longer on the prow, Pleasure no more at the helm. And even as I write, magically another verse comes back to me, typical of the brooding melancholy of the poem.

> No longer drones the drowsy dragon-fly,
>   No longer wheels the swallow in its flight;
> No longer does the tadpole wonder why
>   Its tail began to dwindle in the night.

Recited (as they should be) in the voice usually reserved for the plays of M. Maeterlinck, these lines bring one very close to tears. But it is the last verse which seems to bar the door to all hope, all expectancy. Ranging lightly through the Animal Kingdom I come at last to the dim vegetable world, and so to the inevitable end . . .

> The marigold lies withered in its bed,
>   The solitary tulip-bulb has fused,
> The sycamore is wishing it were dead . . .
>   Even the smilax fails to be amused.

Every now and then at this time of the year, when so many young people have finished their 'education', have had a nice holiday, and are now wondering what to do, I get letters asking me 'how to become a writer'. I gather from these letters that my correspondents know already how to write (and in any case I couldn't tell them much about that); what they want to know now is how to get paid for it. Once I had a letter from a sympathetic father. Fathers are not usually sympathetic; they feel that their sons should be doing a real job of work in an office or the great open spaces, and 'scribbling', if so it pleased them, in their spare time. This one,

to my surprise, was really anxious that his boy should do the
work he wanted to do. In some extraordinary way he had
realized that 'writing' counted as work, and he was now
trying to find out if there was any future in it.

About all these letters there is something of the air of the
dear woman who meets a novelist, wonders if he is 'writing
anything just now', hears with surprise that he is writing a
novel, and asks eagerly where she can get it; I mean the air of
being in the presence of a mystery not subject to natural laws.
Because anybody can buy a pen and, even in these days, a
little paper: because there are no examinations to pass, no
trade unions to join, no hard-earned letters after one's name
to win: the young writer is apt to tell himself that, once one
is born with the gift (as, of course, one is), one has only to
discover the right password, and all doors will be magically
open. But what is the password? How does one get one's
masterpiece accepted by an obviously unlettered editor or
publisher? The merest glance at the work of the chosen tells
one that literary values have no part in the decision. If blackmail is advisable, which editor is the most promising subject?

On these occasions I try to be helpful. For I do feel, just as
genuinely as most of my correspondents seem to, that if I did
it, anybody can do it. This isn't modesty, mock or otherwise.
It springs from a natural distaste for his own Juvenilia which
comes, I suppose, to every writer of my age. 'Surely,' he tells
himself as he looks back on them uneasily, 'nobody could
start with less than that, and hope to make a success of it.'

Most young writers when they begin are either self-conscious and therefore awkward, or consciously modelling what
they think of as their style on the style of some other writer
—and, inevitably, leaving out all that matters, the other
writer's personality. Whatever gifts they bring, they have

still to learn how to display them. In humour, invention, imagination, young A may be ten times more highly endowed than the well-established B ; posterity may be celebrating his centenary when the gravestone is still only remarking that B was respected by all who knew him; yet commonplace B may have something which makes him at the moment more acceptable to editor or publisher, and rightly more acceptable, than gifted A.

What is this something? It is easier to explain it in relation to speaking than to writing. A is a delightful person to talk with, gay, amusing, quick, all that we want in a companion. B is slow, dull, devoid of humour. But let them both address a public meeting, and it is easy to see that B may do it successfully and A be a complete failure. Well, writing, whether for the editor of a school magazine, for a humble living, or for posterity, is addressing a public meeting. However brilliant youth may be, it has still to learn how to 'get over'. A bad actor can fail to do this with Wilde's most brilliant lines; a good actor can do it with a line from which even the author didn't expect a laugh. A writer has to find out his own way of addressing a public meeting, and he can only find it by continuous practice.

Edison called 'genius' one per cent inspiration and ninety-nine per cent perspiration. I don't know anything about genius, but I know that an intolerable deal of perspiration is needed from a writer if he is to make tolerable his one half-pennyworth of inspiration. But are inspiration and perspiration enough? Alas! no; not today. When I began to write, there were eight evening papers in London, all of which printed articles from the unknown free-lance. It is true that they only paid a guinea an article, but it is equally true that an ounce of tobacco and two boxes of matches, which cost

five shillings now, cost fivepence then. Today there are only
three evening papers, and very little room in them for the
outside contributor. There is less paper for publishers; there
is less inducement for an air-conditioned public to read; waiting in the background there is a more grasping Chancellor of
the Exchequer. How, then, does a young man 'become a
writer'?

He doesn't.

Yet if he wants to write, he can write, and nobody and
nothing can stop him. He can become a clergyman, like
Swift; a lawyer, like Scott; a doctor, like Maugham; a Civil
Servant, like Trollope; a schoolmaster, like Wells; a reporter,
like Dickens; an architect, like Hardy—and still write. But it
may be some years before he can sustain himself by creative
writing. Does this matter very much? It does not seem to
have mattered in the past. I shall admit gladly and gratefully
that, when I began to write, conditions were much more merciful to the young than they are today; but not that they are
less merciful now than they were in, say, Jane Austen's time.

But these are the days when private enterprise and (if I may
say so) private guts are discouraged. So it is not surprising
that there is talk in what are called literary circles of State
subsidies for young poets, enabling them to give their full
time at once to young poetry. Yet it is a little eccentric of
those who are most scornful of the public, and whose work
is most obviously designed for private admiration, to assert
thus a right to public support. A State subsidy is not a grant
from his own purse kindly made by a literary Chancellor of
the Exchequer, even though the Cabinet will claim the credit
for it. It is money subscribed reluctantly by the illiterate
public. I can imagine nothing more desiccating to a young
writer than the knowledge that he owes three hundred

pounds' worth of inspiration to people whom he despises, and that payment must be made before the end of the year. A Poet Laureate, with only a butt of sack to account for, is sufficiently embarrassed.

In an earlier chapter I spoke of the pleasant discoveries which an untidy person can make. This morning I came across a letter which I had written on October 13th, 1916, from what was left of a French village called Bully-Grenay. My C.O. was a man for whom I had the greatest admiration, and when he died between the wars, I paid a farewell tribute to him in *The Times*. He had a delightfully ironic humour, of which I gave one or two examples, reminding myself of them by referring to letters which I had written home. This one, however, had escaped me, until today.

There was a certain newly-joined subaltern, a hard-working but extremely unattractive youth, whom I described as 'dry-dirty', whatever that meant. The Colonel and the Adjutant were talking about him in the H.Q. Mess, to which as Signalling Officer I belonged; and the Adjutant said in his kindly way that he was 'a very well-meaning boy, but not exactly a leader.'

'No,' said the Colonel, 'the men would never follow him —except out of curiosity.'

IN November, 1918, Nigel Playfair began rehearsals of his first production at the newly-opened Lyric Theatre, Hammersmith, this being a children's play for which I was partly responsible. My enforced contribution to the publicity on which the Stage revolves was an interview, arranged by the management, in a certain daily paper. The subject chosen by the interviewer was Laughter, it being hoped that I was already, or by this play should prove to be, an authority on its inducement.

We sat in the dress circle and talked quietly, while Playfair conducted the rehearsal from beneath us. In fact, the other man did most of the talking, my share of it being limited to variations on the themes 'Er, yes, in a way' and 'Well, no, not exactly.' A listener-in would have supposed that a rough proof of somebody else's interview was now being read to me, my approval being asked as a matter of courtesy, but not insisted on. But when it appeared next morning it was all in the first person, and I was the speaker.

In 1900 Bergson had published his famous textbook *Le Rire*; eighteen years later I was adding a footnote to it. In the first sentence I was allowed to use the word 'laughter', and I shall always be grateful for this. In the second sentence, not wishing to repeat myself, I spoke of 'the exercise of the risible faculties'. In the third sentence I referred briefly to 'the art of cachinnation'. After this, all that was left for me to say was 'Personally I prefer to use the rapier rather than the bludgeon' . . . and you may be sure that I said it.

When an author gets a reputation for avoiding interviews, it is customary to explain his unnatural conduct in one of two ways. Either he is 'shy and retiring', with a 'genuine horror of publicity'; or else, with a subtlety which (I should have supposed) might easily overreach itself, he is seeking a still greater publicity by exhibiting his distaste for it. The third, and more compelling reason, does not present itself to the lay mind so readily. He is afraid of having the wrong words attributed to him.

Speech is the first rough draft of thought: writing is the laboriously finished product of many drafts. Accurate word-for-word reporting of an interview would be as embarrassing to an author as would be the accidental publication of his first scrawled pencil notes for a story. But in fact no such reporting takes place. All that the interviewer notes is the sense of what is said to him; he himself will supply the words. This matters little to those to whom words matter little. A scientist explaining the hydrogen bomb, or an economist giving his views on inflation, is content if the facts or the views are not misrepresented; but any adumbration of another writer's words misrepresents what matters most to him. There used to be a song with some such refrain as 'It ain't so much the things 'e sez, as the nasty way 'e sez 'em'. Substitute for 'nasty' any adjective you think more suitable, and you are describing almost any writer.

This explains why professional writers make such a poor

showing in Brains Trusts and similar gatherings. It is difficult for one who has spent his whole working life in refining his thoughts for the market to reconcile himself to a hurried, uncorrected version of them. He is as much *en pantoufles*, and conscious of it, as a woman surprised by an influx of visitors when at work in the garden. Justice, they feel, is not being done to them, so how can they do themselves justice? I have never understood why a questioning public, anxious to know which half-a-dozen discs, books or companions members of a B.B.C. team would choose to be wrecked with, is supposed to prefer the answers to be as little considered and as ill phrased as possible. The original Brains Trust was all very well. Knowledge was being sought, and knowledge, accurate or inaccurate, supplied. Why does a horse get up with its forelegs first, when a cow starts with its hindlegs? How does a fly land upside down on the ceiling? What is the difference between the Eastern and Western conception of music? Anybody who thinks he knows the answer can give it at once. But when the Brains Trust dissolved into an Opinions Trust, died, and left behind it a lot of little joint stock companies with nothing but personal preferences for the shareholders, then the old method of unrehearsed question and spontaneous answer had lost its value. A fact is a fact, and no amount of thought or polish will make it anything else; but an opinion is only valuable if it is well considered and well expressed.

In criticizing the B.B.C. one needs to remind oneself constantly that one is not the only listener. I need this reminder more than most people. When I break into the middle of a cricket or football commentary my immediate need is for a full record of the play up to date. Why cannot the commentator leave the uninteresting present for a minute, and give me a quick summary of the past? Has he no consideration for people like myself? But if, when I have been with him from the beginning, he should leave the exciting present in order to play over his well-worn record of the past, I am equally indignant. Why should my time be wasted over an uninteresting summary of what I know so well? It is difficult to be more unreasonable than this, yet I am so unreasonable. I shall continue to be so.

There is something about a communal noise which seems to appeal to many, and ought, I suppose, to appeal to me. If I were to say to a neighbour: 'I have a very long-winded man staying with me, may I bring him round to your house at 9.15 this evening? He wants to tell you about the dollar gap, or a walk he had in Siam, or something. It will take him about twenty minutes, if you don't mind listening in silence for that time,' little enthusiasm would be shown. Indeed, I cannot imagine anybody saying 'How nice!' in a convincing way. But ten million people will listen gladly to him if he is broadcasting. Ten million people, who would never think of reading *Barchester Towers* quietly to themselves, will listen to it 'over the air'. People who had long lost all desire to play the old family game of 'Clumps' get a new vicarious happiness in listening to other people playing it. A play of which they had said, 'Oh, I don't want to see that, I hate *that* sort of play,' when it was running at a theatre, becomes an evening's entertainment when it can be heard not seen.

Why? It isn't enough to answer that they get it for nothing and get it without trouble. I can get a bump on the head for nothing and without trouble in almost any room in this house. Something else calls to them: the marvels of Science; the community feeling that ten million other people are listening too; the comforting thought that now they need not make conversation, need not read, need not do anything; just listen . . .

It is recorded of a certain caterpillar not otherwise eminent in history that, on being asked in what order it put down its legs, it became so confused by its detailed analysis of what had been an instinctive action, that from then onward it was unable to walk at all. Now with educated people reading is as instinctive a process as walking. At a first attempt to analyse it we should be inclined to say that we read by sight. I know a nice woman whose lips form every syllable, and sometimes, if you are close enough, you can actually hear her murmuring the words; she is in fact reading aloud to herself. Most of us, however, read with closed mouths (breathing lightly through the nose), and let the mere sight of the word translate itself into meaning. But is this really what happens? Are we not, in fact, sounding every word within ourselves? No question that we can make these noiseless noises. We can all sing to ourselves in complete silence; indeed, I am, in this mode, one of the most accurate and tuneful singers of my acquaintance. Every note has a bell-like certainty in my mind, and I know at once when I am slightly out of key. It is only when I open my mouth that transmission becomes faulty. In the same way, when we read, we are, we must be, repeating the words to ourselves unconsciously; for how else should we discover, as we have all discovered in our time, that we have been mispronouncing a word which, in fact, we have never spoken?

I refer to such words as 'misled', which I, and millions of others when young, supposed to be 'mizzled'.

But whether we murmur to ourselves, consciously or subconsciously, or read by sight, we let the words do their own work. Now the B.B.C. may be annoying at times (and at times it is very annoying): it may break up this or that happy marriage, by forcing itself on one member of the partnership, or denying itself to the other: but in respect of its newsreading it can be admired without reservation. The criticism, often made, that its readers are toneless, mechanical, without apparent interest in what they are reading, is the highest praise. It is just what they should be.

Consider any representative piece of news as read to us at nine o'clock.

'The Foreign Ministers' deputies held their 45th meeting in Paris yesterday in an attempt to agree upon an agenda. Mr Gromyko was in the chair. The discussion lasted for five hours, and was adjourned until tomorrow. No progress was made.'

Now these words tell their own story (that is what words are for), and no word needs to be coloured, emphasized or picked out in order to make the matter clear to the reader. Imagine it in the Stop Press News, or on the tape in an hotel, imagine your wife asking you to read it out to her, as she hadn't got her spectacles, and then imagine yourself reading it aloud in the colourful voice urged so often on the B.B.C. news-readers: the drawn-out 'forty-fifth', the humorous pause before 'agree', the ironic emphasis of 'discussion', and the final play on the last four words, delivered solemnly or thrown away casually, according to taste. What would happen? Your wife would ring up the doctor at once and say, 'Will you come round and see my husband? Something's gone wrong with him. I think he thinks he's Sir Herbert Tree.' And if we shouldn't tolerate the news given out privately in this way, why should we tolerate it, even delight in it, when coming to us over the air? Aren't we grown up? Don't we understand what simple words mean? Can't we organize our own reactions?

As a writer who loves words and lives by them, I am as jealous for them as is a dog-lover for his friends, and as indignant as he when they are dressed up and put through tricks at a circus. Words need no dressing. In writing dialogue it is sometimes wise to underline, so that the stress comes immediately in the right place; for in dialogue one is circumscribed by the character's choice and arrangement of words, and if he depend upon intonation, so must the author. But in narrative, where the author has a free hand, it should hardly ever be necessary. Let us be grateful to the B.B.C. news-readers that they spare us the italics and exclamation marks with which dear Victorian women sprinkled their letters, a running commentary on the obvious.

And how grateful I should be if singers would sing again. To me the chief horror of crooning is not that it does less than justice to the music, but that it does more than justice to the words. One hears them; one hears the damned things, every syllable of them.

> Neath skies that are blee-oo,
>   Or clouds that are gray,
> I shall be always thinking of ye-oo,
>   And my heart will say:
> 'I shall never forget you!'
> _Ever_ since I first met you,
>   And your little hand stole into mine,
>   I knew that love was divine;
>   Ever since our first kiss,

Which told me that love was like this,
I have been tree-oo
To ye-oo.

I think that that is a fair sample of what a crooner confides to us. If he had sung it in the old way, we should have been listening to the music, heedless of the words; indeed, they would have been happily so mouthed and distorted as to be hardly recognizable. But it is (I suppose) the pride of the crooner that he gets the words over, even if he has to leave the music in order to do so. He takes them, it seems, quite seriously.

Having said this, I remind myself that much of what is called 'popular music', marches, waltzes, and the like, such as gives pleasure to unmusical people like myself, probably nauseates the real music-lover as profoundly as these revelations of a crooner's love-life nauseate the lover of words. There are musical clichés and musical banalities, but we do not recognize them. As against this, there is an ingenious musical device which every writer must have envied in times of stress. I mean the *reprise*. By use of this device a 1,500-word light article in waltz-time would demand a labour equivalent to that of a 500-word article. Each paragraph would automatically be written twice, and, gravelled for lack of matter, one would recur to each of the old paragraphs in turn, blending it with the occasional new one. In a more serious article for the monthly reviews the repetition would not be so obvious, but one would stop from time to time to remind the reader of what he was being reminded, using the same words as often as possible. And when one had said all that one had to say, one wouldn't just stop; on the contrary, one would go on and on, making it quite clear that now it was all over. Perhaps in some such words as these:

'End. Finish. Conclusion. And So To Bed. Finish. Finish. Finish. Finis. End. And . . . So . . . To . . . Bed-d-d-d-d. To bed to bed to bed to bed to bed. To—— Bed!'

At two guineas a thousand it mounts up.

It is a habit of the Englishman to be ashamed of his country's virtues and complacent of her faults; probably because he mistakes the one for the other. In no way does he show this more clearly than in his apologetic attitude to the weather. Not only does he owe his resilience, his humour, his capacity for enduring sudden changes of fortune, his adaptability, and, to come from the abstract to the concrete, the whole British Commonwealth and Empire to the English climate: but he has acquired these benefits while enjoying what, in itself, is the best weather in the world, charged with the best quality in life, variety.

'The idiot who praises every country but his own' will continue to extol every climate but his own. He will tell you of his delightful holidays abroad in this place or that, and of the wonderful weather he had; not realizing that he was carefully sampling it at its own chosen season. 'Have you ever been to New York in the fall?' he will ask. '*There's* weather for you!' But there is also weather in New York in January and July, and of this he knows nothing. We have all had memorable fortnights in Italy, and sent glowing postcards back to damp and dreary friends in London, receiving their envious letters in return; but let us ask any young man who fought through the Italian campaign what he thinks of

Italian weather. He has seen it all, from January to December, and will give us a very different opinion of it. Everybody knows that it never rains in Paris, which is why they have those charming open-air restaurants in the streets, so romantic, so—what is the word we want?—so *Bohemian*, so utterly *French*; yet I can remember a fortnight's continuous rain in France, one October thirty-five years ago, though the natives, maybe, considered that we had brought it with us. Those warm, blue nights in the desert, when sheikhs make love and passionate novels are conceived, they are not always so warm, nor, in any meaning of the word, so blue; and if they were, they would be extremely boring. It is impossible to be bored by any one manifestation of English weather.

Admittedly, however, some foreigners complain of it. This is because, unlike other countries, we have no advertised season. If we could guarantee perfect June weather in June, then, whatever the rest of the year was like, the English climate would have a reputation abroad which would outbid all Festivals and Fun Fairs. 'O to be in England!' would be the cry of sweltering New Yorker and shivering Italian. But because we distribute the weather natural to each month impartially among all the other months, foreigners say what they say . . . and we are what we are.

Continuing to do my best for our weather (and this is the month in which to do it), I shall now mention another of its advantages. Ask any woman which year it was when she went to Chamonix or Cheltenham: what month it was when Mrs Green or the Duchess dropped in to lunch: and she will say at once that long evening dresses were just coming in, or that she was wearing the little flowered cotton. Men's fashions change too slowly to allow them any such aide-mémoire; all that they can say with confidence is that they were wearing a pair of trousers. Sartorially, one year to them is another year; but climatically, years stand out like spires in a crowded city. The winters of 1895, 1902, 1927 and 1939: Augusts of 1893, 1914 and 1932; the May frosts of 1935; the lost spring of 1917, when winter carried over into summer: the summer of 1906, most lovely of all, followed by that of 1907, most unlovely: as we look down the past, first one, then another, takes the eye and stirs the memory. The magic of a February day with a first faint fluttering of April in the air, of an October day when for a few hours August made a shy return, in whatever year they came we shall remember them.

Meteorologists tell us where our weather is coming from, but not where it is going to. So, when we read that a depression is approaching slowly from Iceland, we must not suppose that Icelanders are being told that a depression is departing slowly for England. Once they have finished with their depression, they care not what becomes of it. But no doubt they had been told earlier that this depression was approaching slowly from Greenland. What was Greenland told?

The point I am trying to make is that any dark and depressing day, like this on which I am trying to write, comes from a long way back, both in time and space. Indeed, I see no way of avoiding the deduction that it comes from the beginning of time. For the weather is something, however explained, over which man has no control. Every manifestation of it has a preceding natural cause, which again has a preceding natural cause . . . and so back to the First Cause. It is, I suggest, the complete example of predestination. One can tell oneself that the evolution of animal life, from its first form (sea-slugs) to its latest form (Communists), has not necessarily taken a predestined course. Some power of choice was left to each species; or, if not that, then at least a comforting belief in such power. But there is no escape from the conclusion that today's unpleasant dreariness was determined at the creation of the Universe, and that, for all these millions of years, mankind has been powerless to avert it. In another million years from now we may have progressed sufficiently to say that in another million years from then Englishmen will be having such-and-such weather on such-and-such a day; and yet still be unable to do anything about it.

Except write about it.

Are there any objective or self-existent numbers in Nature? I know not why I should have wondered about this in the war, but I did so wonder; and today, having found an old letter, am wondering again. A number is a multiplication of units, and Man decides what the unit is. The earth is 92 million miles from the sun. Substitute kilometres, versts or parasangs for miles, and the number gives way to another number. There are 24 hours in a day, but an hour is an arbitrary division of time; invented by Man, who is now responsible for the '24'. A cow by any other name would still have 4 legs, but, if it were an insect, it would have 6, and, if a bird, 2. Are there any absolute numbers for which Nature alone is responsible?

Writing to Eddington about something else, I asked him the question. I asked with some diffidence, as humbly aware as any schoolboy that I might be making myself ridiculous;

hearing in imagination the loud sycophantic laugh from the whole form, as the curl of the master's lip indicated that laughter would be in place. Even if the question were sensible, it might be as naïvely misdirected to The Observatory, Cambridge, as would be a question on the difference between a reef-knot and a granny (stamped addressed envelope enclosed) to The Admiralty, London.

So it was a relief to get an answer which began 'The numbers in Nature is a theme on which I could talk for hours,' even though it continued 'I regard 5 as rather a third-rate number.' For 5 had seemed to me the nearest approach to an absolute number, and I had put it forward hopefully. I must have had a good reason at the time, but now I go about muttering 'Why did I say five?' Don't let anybody suggest that it was because we have 5 fingers and 5 toes. Nobody with my devotion to crosswords could have failed to remember the Ai or Two-Toed Sloth. Why five? If any Fellow of the Royal Society can lower his mind for a moment to the level of mine, and tell me what makes us both think of 5, I shall be glad to hear from him.

To return to Eddington. He went on:

The parent number is 4, and his principal offspring are 3, 10, 136, 137, $2 \times 136 \times 2^{256}$. But I don't think there are any fundamental numbers in Nature. . . . My own favourite is 137. In atomic physics it is known as the fine-structure constant: and in the last 12 years I have watched the experimental values, starting about 136·5, getting closer and closer, till the latest is 137·009.

Well, you see what he means; or, if you don't, you are seeing exactly what I saw. I had gone for a pleasant little paddle in a pleasantly speculative little sea, and now the waters were swirling over my head, and my feet, 5 toes on each, were feeling vainly for standing-ground.

With the last paragraph I was swept back into my own depth.

Of course, I recognise that there *are* numbers in Nature that we do not put in ourselves, *e.g.* numbers of planets in the solar system. But these are casual numbers. My conclusion is concerned only with fundamental numbers.

I can understand that. But if the number of planets were the same for every solar system, then that number (surely ?) would be fundamental. As it is, all I shall assert is that 2 is absolute. Everything is or is not. But I still feel that there was something to be said for 5, if only I could remember what it was.

We all called him Bill, though that was not his real name. He had a travelling acquaintance with most of the arts, and from one of them, the art of writing, made a living. But his knowledge seemed to embrace every activity of mankind, great and small. If you wanted to know how to get from London to Lhasa most quickly, who invented the first bicycle, or when wimples went out of fashion, he would tell you. Once, when I was sitting in the lounge of the club, I heard, but without recognition, two voices descending the stairs. While they were still out of sight, one voice was saying to the other: 'If you look a tiger firmly in the eye . . .' and unhesitatingly I murmured 'Bill.' It was Bill. I could not doubt that at some time in his various life he had so regarded a tiger, and, emerging scatheless, had added another morsel of information to his encyclopaedic store. It seemed that he knew everything.

One morning, when Bill's versatility was still holding surprises for me, I was there in the lounge, listening to an idle talk about the state of St. Paul's Cathedral. *The Times* had just opened a fund for repair work to its foundations, which were causing alarm to the Dean and Chapter. Somebody was wondering what all the fuss was about. Fortunately Bill was with us to give the answer. He explained most interestingly about the different strata in the make-up of London soil, he spoke at length of diluvial fissure and subterranean springs. I was fascinated. Still talking, he led the way into the coffee-room, followed by most of the others. One man, who had been as silent as myself, was left behind.

I said, a note of envy in my voice, 'I didn't know Bill knew so much about geology.'

He looked up and said: 'Bill? He doesn't know a thing about geology.'

I was a little hurt by this. I felt that Bill's universal knowledge was something of which the Club should be proud. I said coldly:

'How do you know? Are *you* a geologist?'

He seemed surprised. He said: 'Oh no, no, good heavens, no. I'm a botanist.'

'Then how on earth——' I began indignantly.

'Well, you see,' he smiled, 'I once heard Bill talking about botany.'

This I feel is a warning to all of us.

It was some months later, when interesting facts about coats-of-arms were floating down the long table to us, that one of the oldest members said to me in his precise little voice: 'I think Bill has the greatest fund of inaccurate information of anybody I know.' It was a hard thing to say of so engaging a man, but no doubt he was a palaeontologist, and had once heard Bill talking of palaeontology.

CHARLES STUART CALVERLEY was born on December 17th, 1831. He was the supreme master of one of the loveliest of arts: an art, even at its most popular, practised by few and appreciated by not many more: now a dying art, having such exigent laws, and making such demands on the craftsmanship of its practitioners, that it has no place in a brave, new, unperspiring world: the Art of Light Verse.

I propose to be so old-fashioned as to write in praise of it.

Light Verse obeys Coleridge's definition of poetry, the best words in the best order; it demands Carlyle's definition of genius, transcendent capacity of taking pains; and it is the supreme exhibition of somebody's definition of art, the concealment of art. In the result it observes the most exact laws of rhyme and metre as if by a happy accident, and in a sort of nonchalant spirit of mockery at the real poets who do it on purpose. But to describe it so leaves something unsaid; one must also say what it is not. Light Verse, then, is not the relaxation of a major poet in the intervals of writing an epic; it is not the kindly contribution of a minor poet to a little girl's album; it is not Cowper amusing (and how easily)

Lady Austin, nor Southey splashing about, to his own great content, in the waters of Lodore. It is a precise art which has only been taken seriously, and thus qualified as an art, in the nineteenth and twentieth centuries. It needs neither genealogical backing nor distinguished patronage to make it respectable.

From time to time anthologies of light verse are produced. The trouble with most of the anthologists is that, even if they have an understanding of their subject, secretly they are still a little ashamed of it. They try to give it the blessings of legitimacy by tracing its ancestry back to some dull fourteenth-century poem beginning 'Lhude sing cuccu' or 'Merry swithe it is in halle'. If any intervening major poet (other than Byron) has unbent for a moment, the distressing result is dragged in, to provide the sanction of respectability which the Vicar brings to the raffle at the Choirboys' Outing. 'Poets at Play' said one anthologist, and we see at once that there is no real harm in it. One mustn't take them seriously, it's only their fun.

Now if anybody wishes to see what happens when a poet is at play, he has only to read that most deplorable piece of doggerel, *John Gilpin*. Light Verse is not the output of poets at play, but of light-verse writers (who would not thank you today for calling them poets) at the hardest and most severely technical work known to authorship. It is not bastard poetry on a frivolous theme. It is true humour expressing itself in perfectly controlled rhyme and rhythm.

The pattern of light verse is to be found in Calverley. Before I begin to quote from him—and once I begin, I may find it difficult to stop—I shall contrast four lines from *John Gilpin* with four lines from *The Hunting of the Snark*, the difference between them exhibiting to perfection the first necessary quality of light verse, naturalness of rhyme and rhythm.

Cowper wrote:

> Quoth Mrs Gilpin 'That's well said;
> And for that wine is dear,
> We will be furnished with our own
> Which is both bright and clear.'

Of course Mrs Gilpin quoth nothing of the sort. When recommending a wine, one advances something more in its favour than that it is 'both bright and clear'; nor was it likely that Gilpin knew less about the wine in his cellar than his wife, and needed the information. What she really said (in prose) was: 'A very good idea; and since all these inns, and I don't suppose the Bell is any exception, overcharge ridiculously, we'd better take our own wine with us.' Cowper had to translate this into verse. In the result the words are unnatural, the scansion is strained, and the first and third lines do not rhyme, as in light verse they should. In fact, the speech as translated has nothing to recommend it, save that it can just qualify as verse by reason of having the right number of feet and a rhyme for the second and fourth lines. But it is not light verse. It is very heavy verse. We are told that Cowper 'jotted it down during a sleepless night', 63 verses of it. It bears all the signs of having been jotted down . . .

I have now amused myself by making my own translation of Mrs Gilpin's speech. Here it is. It has faults of its own, no doubt: an excess of frivolity, perhaps: but it obeys the rules. It is 'light verse' in its own right; not merely light because the subject is light, or because I didn't work at it seriously.

> Said Mrs Gilpin: 'Very well.
> But wait a moment! What'll
> They charge for claret at the Bell?
> We'd better take a bottle.'

I apologize for intruding myself on the stage when I have Lewis Carroll waiting in the wings. Here is a verse from *The Hunting of The Snark*, describing one of the crew when he joined the ship.

> He had forty-two boxes, all carefully packed,
>   With his name painted clearly on each;
> But since he omitted to mention the fact,
>   They were all left behind on the beach.

Now nothing could be more delightfully natural than that. There is neither a wrong word in it, nor a right word misplaced. But that sort of naturalness comes by prayer and fasting, with blood and sweat and tears. As Sheridan implied, easy reading makes curst hard writing; it cannot be 'dashed off'.

Earlier in this book I wrote in Quiller Couch's phrase, of the Great Thrill in poetry. Light verse in its different way can produce its own Great Thrill for those who appreciate its ardours: a shock of delighted surprise, sometimes at an unexpected rhyme: an effect which Calverley gets so happily by a sudden breakdown from a mocked high-falutery to a deliberate matter-of-factness.

> Ere the morn the East has crimsoned,
>   When the stars are twinkling there
> (As they did in Watts's hymns, and
>   Made him wonder what they were):
> When the forest nymphs are beading
>   Fern and flower with silvery dew—
> My infallible proceeding
>   Is to wake and think of you.

As Wordsworth said: Dull would he be of soul who could pass by a verse so perfect in its mockery.

Here are two other examples:

> O my earliest love, who, ere I numbered
>   Ten sweet summers, made my bosom thrill!
> Will a swallow—or a swift or some bird—
>   Fly to her and say I love her still? . . .
>
> O my earliest love, still unforgotten,
>   With your downcast eyes of dreamy blue!
> Never, somehow, could I seem to cotton
>   To another as I did to you.

And

> Oh sweet—as to the toilworn man
>   The far-off sound of rippling river;
> As to cadets in Hindostan
>   The fleeting remnant of their liver——

In the last example the breakdown is the more happy for being humorous in itself; as also in this:

> Once, a happy child, I carolled
>   O'er green lawns the whole day through,
> Not unpleasingly apparelled
>   In a tightish suit of blue.

In *Lovers, and a Reflection* the mockery is more particularly aimed; this time at the drawing-room ballad of those days: sung by eligible young men, who were reminded to bring their music with them when asked out to dinner.

> In moss-prankt dells which the sunbeams flatter
>   (And Heaven it knoweth what that may mean;
> Meaning, however, is no great matter)
>   Where woods are a-tremble with rifts atween ;
>
> Through God's own heather we wonn'd together,
>   I and my Willie (O love, my love!):
> I need hardly remark it was glorious weather,
>   And flitterbats waver'd alow, above: . . .

Through the red heather we danced together
(O love, my Willie!) and smelt for flowers:
I must mention again it was gorgeous weather,
Rhymes are so scarce in this world of ours——

After they had 'thrid God's cowslips as erst his heather',
then 'Willie gan sing'; and in his song

Mists, bones, the singer himself, love-stories
And all least furlable things got 'furled';
Not with any design to conceal their 'glories',
But simply and solely to rhyme with 'world'.

And so to the Reflection.

O if billows and pillows and hours and flowers
And all the brave rhymes of an elder day,
Could be fitted together, this genial weather
And carted or carried on 'wafts' away,
Nor ever again trotted out—ah me!
How much fewer volumes of verse there'd be!

But Calverley didn't know what was coming. If he had,
his last verse might have been this:

When rhyme and any discernible rhythm,
Victorian chains, are filed away,
And form and grammar and sense go with'em,
Those harsh restraints of an elder day,
And 'inspiration' at last is free,
How packed with 'poets' the world will be!

But even he couldn't have parodied them.

Until today we had four cats. Now we have only three, for Cleopatra has left us. She was a small gracious creature, and there was a time when she favoured me above all others in the household, joining me in a dignified yet purposeful way whenever she saw me in the garden. But the cares of family life gradually estranged her. Four kittens every three months leave one little time for the social amenities.

Caesar was her brother: a grey like herself, very loving of his mistress, and with no pretence to beauty. He has spent most of his life as an uncle, and two of his nephews are with us now: Wog II, a big black cat with white paws, waistcoat and whiskers, and the much younger Bimbo. Bimbo will be the handsomest of all, striped with geometrical precision, but not yet grown to the length of his tail, nor aware that as a foursome partner on the putting-lawn he is out of place.

Caesar and Wog II are the great hunters. They catch moles and rabbits, rats and mice; and if at times they leave the less digestible portions in the library, well, one cannot expect them to have the feeling for books which others have. Constant head-smacking has reduced their ardour for birds; the occasional lizard gets away in the end (the front end) leaving, without apparent regret, the tail end behind him. Bimbo is still young enough to be interested in bees, an interest which time and the bees will soon dispel. When he is seen with a mouse, it may be his own, or he may have taken it over from Caesar, for whom mice are very small game. Cleopatra, as I have said, is exclusively a mother.

We had been accustomed to drown three of Cleo's kittens as soon as they arrived, leaving the fourth to comfort her. By the time it was old enough for adoption, four more would be on the way. We had hoped that Cleo would not have felt deeply about this, but it must have been preying on her mind through many sessions in the basket, and at last she decided that action was needed. Once more the basket was prepared for her . . . once more the hour approached . . . and now there was no Cleopatra. . . .

Two days later she returned to us, lean and hungry. But where was the new family? The attics were searched; each improbable cupboard was explored; the library, naturally, was examined, almost book by book. No kittens. Stoked up with fish and milk, Cleopatra disappeared again, returning next morning for another day's rations. This time she was followed out of the house, at first openly (but she knew all about that), then more secretly. It was an hour before the kittens were located, many hours before they were recovered. For she had climbed twenty feet up an old ivy-clad walnut-tree, and made a nest there for herself and her family. Twenty feet higher up two wood-pigeons were nesting. The cat among the pigeons; a lass, we felt, unparalleled.

As a reward for her motherly devotion she was allowed to keep two of the family this time. One of them was Bimbo, which may account for the ramifications of his coat; with difficulty we found a home for the other. For alas! the supply of kittens was so quickly exceeding the demand that Cleo's place in society was no longer assured. Two families later we had taken the great decision. It was a sad one to take, but she had been living in a world of her own for so long that all personal relationship with her had lapsed. So today Cleopatra has left us for another home, where her passing, I feel sure, will be as painless and as dignified as was her illustrious archetype's.

When the war was just ending, and before we knew what was to follow it, I was asked by an American editor to write an article on such minor pleasures of Peace as I was now hoping to experience. The request came six months too late. I had already experienced them. They had been showered upon us in the previous autumn.

1. The cessation of flying-bombs. We are in a direct line from Dieppe to London, and they had rattled overhead day and night, just missing the hills on each side of us. Two of them had not missed.

2. The end of the black-out.

3. The dissolution of the Home Guard.

Of the three the last had brought the greatest relief. It was not that I was inapt for military duties. In four years of the First War I had risen like a rocket from Second Lieutenant to Full Lieutenant; and in the four years of the Home Guard, even though starting this time as the rankest of Other Ranks, I had again shot up to Lieutenant. What had got me down was the perpetual struggle on early winter mornings with the car which conveyed me to my duties.

I still struggle, but now only for pleasure; and not on these early winter mornings.

Although the Second Gardener's sole duty to me is to garden, as mine to him is to pay his wages, sometimes we do a little for each other on the side. Thus, on one day he will call me in to explain one of those intriguing forms without which we should all fare so much less well, if so much more happily; and on another I shall be asking him casually to come and give the car a wind, the self-starter having once again failed to start anything but itself. To each according to his need, from each according to his capacity. I provide the brains, he the brawn.

He is not a natural car-winder, and the car, being now in its seventeenth winter, does little to encourage him. I do the best I can with choke and accelerator, suggestions that he should try more of a jerk and assurances that we nearly got it that time, but the issue remains uncertain. At our last session we had just given up hope, so that after ten minutes of miscellaneous noises I was saying, 'Oh, well, never mind, I can walk,' when the engine suddenly came to life. He straightened himself with the air of a man who had thought that he would never be straight again, panted a little, and said:

'Mr Parsley up the hill got a new Camelot last week for six hundred pound——'

I bowed my head in shame on the dashboard of my 1935 model. There was no need for him to go on; I saw his point. For the sake of a few miserable pounds I was straining his heart and stimulating his lumbago, while the more generous-minded Mr Parsley up the hill was denying himself a dozen little luxuries simply to keep his gardener in good condition. What Mr Parsley in his less desirable residence (so far, any-way, as chrysanthemums went) had so nobly done, surely I could do. But could I? I had been third on the list for a new car four years ago, and had been ploughing my way steadily downwards ever since. What more was expected of me? I was about to ask him this, when he went on:

'Six hundred pound, and on Saturday morning it took him three hours to start it.'

We beamed at each other. If Mr Parsley (whom I have not had the pleasure of meeting) had been among those present, I should have beamed at him too. I liked his spirit. Note the words 'it took him three hours to start it'; not, as one might have expected, 'he spent three hours trying to start it.' A lesser man might have given up after two hours fifty-nine minutes, but not Mr Parsley. He had resolved to start the car, and he did start the car. He had told himself, and how truly, that in order to get full satisfaction from the road-performance of his new Camelot he must first get it on to the road. The minor satisfactions of mentioning casually to his friends that he had been down for a new Camelot since 1940, and had now been lucky enough to get the one which had been reserved for a man of the same name in the Ministry of Fuel and Power; of taking a visitor round the garden, throwing open the garage doors as if in search of yesterday's *Times*, and saying in surprise, 'Oh, are you looking at my new car?': even the satisfaction of actually sitting in the car, and turning, if it had one, the wireless on: all these were very well, but still something was lacking. Mr Parsley knows what it is. He switches off the Rumbo Jumbo Rhythm Boys, and pulls out the self-starter. For a little while the noises seem much the same. Three hours later . . .

I like his spirit. When we have located 'up the hill' a little more definitely, we must ask him in for a drink: not forgetting, of course, to give him three hours' notice. We must then have a long talk about cars, a subject which I have avoided hitherto. If he should be kind enough to return our hospitality, we can be with him at any time, any time, my dear Parsley, within ten minutes or so, and have another long talk about cars. Mr Parsley—bless him and the whole Camelot organization—had removed an inferiority complex which was doing myself, and possibly the Second Gardener, no good.

For I had had the unworthy conviction that I was the only man in Sussex for whom cars did not start. In the pre-Parsley era, whenever we were rung up and invited to a neighbour's, the automatic acceptance would be 'Delighted, if the car will start'; whereas the acceptance of our return invitation was just 'Delighted'. It was not that other cars were always newer or of superior make, for we have had some very odd-looking specimens parked round the dove-cot; but that the owners had some trick, some ingratiating manner with the machinery of starting, which I lacked. This made me feel even less like the hero of a modern adventure story than my inability to drink beer in large quantities—or, for that matter, and to bring my asthenia more nearly home to American readers, whisky.

But now, it was clear, my humility had been out of place. Two days later I had further confirmation of this.

As anybody with my experience knows, cars start more easily when they are warm than when they are cold. However often our acceptance of an invitation to cocktails had been provisional, there was nothing provisional about our departure. Neither we nor our hosts had ever had any fear that we should be staying to dinner. But now, and for the first time, a half-hour's wait outside a dentist's at our nearest town had so chilled the engine that communication between the self-starter and the works seemed to have closed down for good. Fortunately a real chauffeur, also waiting for a patient, had parked his car next to mine. With my hand in the breast of my coat, and the air of one whose wrist was still giving him trouble, and who had rather stupidly forgotten to bring his Second Gardener with him, I asked if he would be so kind as to—— He sprang from his car with a pleasant, perhaps slightly condescending, smile. 'Right you are, sir,' he said cheerfully, as I handed him the starting-handle. . . . When his mistress tottered out five minutes later, his red face was still coming periodically up over the top of the bonnet for air. He rushed back to open his own door for her, rushed back to my car, and with one supreme effort jerked the engine into life. Before I could move, he had leapt into his seat and driven off.

I put the half-crown back into my pocket. I wished he had stayed to take it, for the pleasure of watching him had been well worth the money.

Some years ago an actor friend of ours, who had disappeared from our lives by retiring into Devonshire, surprised us with a letter. It began:

'I am seventy today. It is an extraordinary age for a young man to be.'

By the time this book appears I shall be seventy; and I feel as bewildered as he was. It is indeed an extraor inary age to be: an age at which, without conscious effort, one should be clothed with dignity and authority; and here am I, invested with neither.

Running an eye over the Engaged column in *The Times*, today or any day, I see that George Pumphrey Baverstock is to be married to Lilian Grace Wetherby; and I say to myself: 'G. P. Baverstock? That must be the man who had rooms over me at Cambridge. Yes, I remember now, the 'P' did stand for Pumphrey. Tall and rather stooping, with a little wisp of black moustache, played lacrosse or some improbable game, we didn't have much to do with each other except for borrowing crockery and things, but I seem to remember rather liking the man. So he's getting married?

Well, well, good luck to him. Wonder what he'd think if I sent him a telegram?'

And then I pull myself together and say, 'Fool! This must be Baverstock's grandson.'

Of course this is only a passing madness. In a general way I realize how old my contemporaries are. I meet one of them and we tell each other that poor old Carnaby—have you seen him lately? You'd hardly recognize him, he looks about a hundred—and Frensham, you remember Frensham?—ran into him the other day at Lord's—simply couldn't believe it when he told me who he was, practically doddering, and he was a couple of years after us. It's very odd, *I* don't feel at all old, do you?—oh, but *you're* marvellous—my dear man, so are you, *exactly* the same. . . . And then we part, and I go home thinking, 'Poor old fellow, *he* won't be with us much longer,' which, no doubt, is just what he is thinking of me.

When I was thirteen years old, my great-great-aunt Garland died. We had never met. Indeed, I had not then heard of her, nor she of me; which was a pity from my point of view, for she was just the sort of great-great-aunt of whom a schoolboy would have liked to boast. Her husband had fought at Trafalgar. This sounds unlikely, but then she died at what would be called the ripe old age of 106. So she was sixteen at that moment of victory, and he—a sub-lieutenant, I suppose—was twenty. He died, a captain, at sixty-five, a long life by the reckoning of those days, yet leaving her with forty-five years of widowhood. There must be many still living who knew her: to whom, perhaps, she had said: 'I remember James telling me that when they heard in his ship that Lord Nelson was dead——' Or even, 'Yes, dear, it was a great shock to us all, but of course a wonderful victory. I remember buying myself a little flag, and waving it at our garden gate to all the passers-by. No, I never met Lady Hamilton myself, naturally I shouldn't have been allowed to at my age, but one of James's shipmates——'

She might have spoken so to me.

When I am 106, I shall be more considerate of my great-great-nephews. I shall keep in touch with them. But what shall I be able to tell them which will lift them above their fellows?

'Yes, I was at Gladstone's funeral in the Abbey, and I remember walking out behind Henry Irving. No, my boy, no relation to 'Lefty' Gladstone the boxer, he was a states-man, leader of the Liberals as they called them then. Irving was a famous actor before the days of television. My memory is not so goo as it was, but I don't *think* he was ever in Twenty Questions, he went in for Shakespeare more.'

Not very interesting. Of course I could talk of the First World War, but there will be plenty of young fellows in the eighties who can tell them all about that.

I am reminded of *The Fugger News-Letters* (1568–1606), and of a particular one from an Italian correspondent which begins quite simply:

Cenci's children were executed here yesterday.

One realizes sadly that this is the only way in which to begin a letter. What one needs in the opening sentence is something of the quality which all good actors have, and all bad actors have not: 'attack'. How void of attack are our ordinary openings:

> I hope you are quite well . . .
> It is ages since I wrote to you . . .

Or, more informatively:

> It has been raining all day.

A friend of mine did assure me that he had once had a letter beginning 'Yesterday I was struck by lightning,' which is good as far as it goes; but it is a little lacking in general interest. Still, one must do what one can with what news one has.

DEAR HENRY,

Yesterday my wife ran away with a Chartered Accountant. It has been a great shock to me, because I didn't know she knew any chartered accountants.

Anybody can see that this is much better than

DEAR HENRY,

I am shocked to have to tell you that my wife ran away yesterday with a Chartered Accountant.

With a woman writing, whose only punctuation mark was a comma, one would expect something like this:

DARLING ELEANOR,

I hope your indigestion is better, I have a nasty cold, I'm sorry to say, my husband left me yesterday, for the girl in the post office——

——leaving Eleanor a little uncertain with which misfortune she was being invited to sympathize.

But I see now that it was unfair to quote the Cenci letter as a model. Nothing which we write will be of general interest until it is become History, and History is not written on the morning after. It is possible that the Italian correspondent had received a letter which said, 'Let me know when Cenci's children are executed,' and was now giving the routine answer, 'Cenci's children were executed yesterday.' It is only after many years that we are thrilled by the realization that this was *the* Cenci. How commonplace in comparison seems our modern, 'It has been raining all day'; yet how thrilling a letter so beginning would be if it were dated approximately 3000 B.C. and signed 'Japheth'. . . .

As I was saying a little while ago, I am on the verge of seventy, and don't feel it. Somebody (it may have been myself) put out the ingenious theory that the reason why actors and actresses continue to look so young is because the hours when they are being Julius Caesar or Little Lord Fauntleroy are no part of their own lives, and so do not age them. Thus an actor who had played Hamlet for eight performances a week throughout the year would himself have lived only forty-five weeks, assuming that he kept his mind on his part during the dressing-room intervals. Continuous employment would give him back one year in eight. Now that I have worked it out, I can see that the theory is not very sound; for an actor is far from being in continuous employment, and even if he were, he would only look forty-two when he was forty-eight, which anybody can do.

But it might apply to a novelist, who does live continuously the lives of others, and perhaps only grows old in the night. It is more likely, however, that the reason why a writer does not easily acquire the dignity and authority of old age is that he is never in a position of dignity or authority. Indeed, he never gets beyond the apprentice stage. When judges, clergymen and schoolmasters open their lips, no dog can bark. Not that any dog wants to; it is assumed (a little too readily, perhaps,) that a Judge knows all about the law, a clergyman all about God, and a schoolmaster all about the subject he is teaching. But however long a writer has been in the business, he is still without authority for anybody but himself. All he knows is how to write in his own way. He will never be Sir Oracle, and any dog can bark at him.

When I wrote an autobiography twelve years ago, I called it *It's Too Late Now*, meaning that it was too late then to be any other sort of writer; no doubt at 106 it will still be too late. The American editor who published it in monthly instalments altered the title. This is a habit of American editors. I fancy that the Oath of Installation—taken (as I see it) in shirt sleeves, elastically banded, with blue pencil upheld in right hand—ends, 'And I do solemnly swear that, whatever the author shall have called any story, article or poem submitted to me, and however suitable his title shall be, I will immediately alter it to one of my own choosing, thus asserting by a single stroke the dignity of my office and my own independence.' However this may be, the autobiography was re-titled 'What Luck!'

I was annoyed with the Editor at the time; but looking back on my life from what I suppose I must call early middle age, I am inclined now to agree with him.